The Mongol Empire

THE MONGOL EMPIRE

First edition. January 23, 2024.

Copyright © 2024 History Nerds.

ISBN: 979-8224411030

Written by History Nerds.

Also by History Nerds

Ancient Empires
The Ottoman Empire
Rome: The Rise and Fall
The Mongol Empire

Celtic Heroes and Legends
Celtic History
William Butler Yeats: Nobel Prize Winning Poet
Robert the Bruce
Scáthach
Finn McCool
William Wallace: Scotland's Great Freedom Fighter

Frauen des Krieges
Boudica: Königin der Icener
Jeanne d'Arc
Irena Sendler

Great Wars of the World
World War 1
World War 2
The Napoleonic Wars: One Shot at Glory
The Serbian Revolution: 1804-1835
Peace Won by the Saber: The Crimean War, 1853-1856
The Fiery Maelstrom of Freedom
The Wars of the Roses

Pirate Chronicles
Grace O'Malley: The Pirate Queen of Ireland
Blackbeard
William Kidd
Ching Shih

The History of the Vikings
Vikings
Longships on Restless Seas

Women of War
Boudica: Queen of the Iceni
Joan of Arc
Irena Sendler
Virginia Hall
Queen Amanirenas

World History
The History of the United Kingdom
The History of Ireland
The History of America
The History of Scotland
The History of Wales

Standalone
Grace O'Malley: Die Piratenkönigin von Irland

Table of Contents

Introduction

"I am the punishment of God...If you had not committed great sins, God would not have sent a punishment like me upon you." - Genghis Khan

With these chilling words, the self styled scourge of God himself articulated a fate that once seemed as inevitable as the rising sun over the vast steppes of Central Asia. Ponder for a moment, what colossal sins could have birthed such a relentless force? This question is not just rhetorical; it's the gateway to understanding the juggernaut that was the Mongol Empire. Imagine an expanse of land so wide, its borders dissolved into the horizon, bound neither by river nor mountain. Here, an epic saga unfolded, one where the thunder of ten thousand hooves became the heartbeat of an empire. But what does it mean for us today? Why should the echoes of ancient conquests trouble the modern mind? Through the swirling sands of the Gobi, amidst whispers of strategy and the clang of steel, an empire rose so swiftly that it seemed conjured by sorcery. Yet, its fall was as mortal as the men who forged it. Within these pages lies not just a tale of power, but of the delicate threads of governance and the brittle nature of domination. Can the rise and fall of the Mongol Empire offer us a mirror to our own world? Will history's warnings resonate in the chambers of current power, or will they be drowned out by the clamor of progress? One thing is certain: in the echoes of the past, there are lessons...

Thunderous hooves and the haunting reverberations of conquest; they resonate across the centuries, a reminder of a time when the world seemed to tremble under the power of one empire. "I am the punishment of God...If you had not committed great sins, God would not have sent a punishment like me upon you." The words of Genghis Khan, fierce and unyielding, set the stage for our exploration into what was the Mongol Empire. But why delve into this chapter of history? What can the meteoric rise and eventual fall of such a power teach us?

The Mongol Empire, in its breadth and scope, challenges our perception of what is possible. It stretched from the Pacific shores of Asia to the heart of Europe, a domain so large that its ruler, the Great Khan, commanded the sun never to set on his domain. Yet, in this vastness lies an intimate tale of humanity: ambition, innovation, cruelty, and the unquenchable thirst for power.

Do we not see reflections of the same desires in today's world leaders and power brokers? The Mongol legacy prompts us to question the nature of power and its impact on the human spirit. It provokes a deeper inquiry into the essence of civilization itself. Is it a force for unity, or an agent of destruction?

As we dissect the anatomy of the Mongol conquests, we uncover a paradox. Here was an empire built on the backs of nomadic horsemen, not the expected pillars of agriculture or sedentary life. How could a society, seemingly so simple in structure, orchestrate a symphony of war and governance that would forever alter the world's geopolitical landscape?

In the narrative of the Mongols, common beliefs about the "barbarian" are turned on their head. They were not merely a horde of savages; they were innovators, statesmen, and strategists. Their military tactics were revolutionary, their religious tolerance was unprecedented, and their impact on trade and culture was transformative.

What then, is the insight that 'History Nerds' brings to these weathered pages of the past? It is the recognition of the Mongol Empire as more than a mere war machine; it was a complex, adaptive force that shaped the world in ways that still resonate. It is a tale of contrasts: brutality coupled with benevolence, conquest with culture, fear with fascination.

Consider your own understanding of empire and leadership. How often do you encounter a narrative that defies the binary of good versus evil, to reveal the multifaceted nature of power? As you turn these pages, allow your curiosity to guide you through the steppes and cities that once trembled at the name of Genghis Khan.

Picture the yurt of a Mongol warrior, the silk-laden markets of Samarkand, the besieged walls of Baghdad. Feel the tension of a world in flux, the uncertainty of an age where the fate of nations was decided in a single battle.

And what of the empire's decline? In its falling, we find the universal truth that nothing, no matter how grand, is immune to the ravages of time and the corrosion of complacency. The Mongol Empire's dissolution serves as a poignant reminder that the seeds of downfall are often sown at the height of triumph.

As the introduction closes, one might ponder: What defines an empire's legacy? Is it the territory conquered or the cultures assimilated? Is it the fear instilled in enemies or the admiration earned from allies? The Mongol story is rich with such questions, and as you embark on this historical journey, be prepared for revelations that will challenge your preconceptions and expand your understanding of what it means to rise, conquer, and ultimately, to fall.

The echoes of the past call to us, and it is our task to listen, learn, and remember. The story of the Mongol Empire is not just a chronicle of a bygone era; it is a narrative that continues to shape our present and our future. Will you heed its call?

The Genesis of Conquest

Before Temujin: The Mongol Tribes

Picture a land of harsh extremes, where the severe cold bites with the ferocity of a wolf and the sprawling steppe stretches to the ends of the earth. This is the cradle of nomadic civilizations, a place where only the most resilient survive and thrive. Here, long before the thunderous conquests of Genghis Khan, a multitude of Mongol tribes roamed the vast grasslands, their lives entwined with the land and the seasons.

In these times of seeming isolation, great movements stirred beneath the surface, shifts that would eventually lead to the emergence of one of history's most formidable empires. The tribes of the Mongolian plateau were as varied as the landscape they inhabited. Each had its own customs, alliances, and rivalries, woven into a delicate tapestry of survival and supremacy.

Why, you might ask, does this era of fragmented clans hold significance for us today? The answer lies in the intricate dance of human interaction, the ebb and flow of conflict and cohesion that preludes any great unification. It is the story of how disparate people can forge a collective identity, a narrative that resonates with any society facing the challenges of division and the quest for harmony.

As the sun rises over the steppe, casting long shadows from the gers dotting the landscape, we sense the dawn of something momentous. The Mongol tribes, though distinct, shared certain traits that sowed the seeds for their eventual amalgamation. Their lives were shaped by the rhythms of pastoral nomadism, their wealth measured in herds of horses, sheep, and goats. In this world, a man's repute was earned through prowess in hunting, horsemanship, and warfare.

In examining the political landscape, we unveil a hierarchy based on kinship and merit, with the tribe led by a khan chosen for his ability to protect and expand the clan's influence. These leaders were adept at forging alliances through marriage, tribute, or the threat of force. Yet, such alliances were as fluid as the rivers that wound their way through the grasslands, often shifting with the fortunes of war and trade.

The Mongols were traders as well as raiders, their horses carrying them across vast distances to exchange goods with neighboring peoples. Through these interactions, ideas flowed as freely as merchandise, and the tribes slowly began to absorb a wider world view. They encountered traders from the Silk Road, adventurers from distant lands, and emissaries from powerful empires.

What lessons do these accounts of tribal life and diplomacy offer us in the modern age? Perhaps it is the understanding that unity often arises from diversity, that strength is born from the ability to adapt and synthesize disparate elements. In our present world, where global issues demand cooperative solutions, the Mongol tribes' journey toward unification provides a compelling blueprint.

As we delve deeper into the fabric of these tribes, we recognize that their customs, while unique, also shared similarities that hinted at a common origin. Marriages were arranged to strengthen clan bonds, and feasts were held to celebrate victories or honor the dead. In the heart of every ger, a fire burned, the family gathering around it to share meals and tales of the day's exploits.

Could the men and women of these tribes have foreseen the future that awaited them? Did they sense the winds of change that would one day coalesce their fates into the hands of a singular leader, Temujin, known to the world as Genghis Khan? These questions linger as we contemplate the remarkable transformation of loosely connected tribes into an empire that would dominate the known world.

It is in the exploration of this pre-Temujin era that we lay the groundwork for understanding the Mongol Empire's rise. From the intricate web of tribal politics to the shared cultural practices, we begin to see the outline of a people poised for greatness. The story of the Mongol tribes is not one of inevitable destiny but of potential, harnessed through the vision and ruthlessness of a leader who would redefine the course of history.

As this chapter draws to a close, we stand at the cusp of an extraordinary narrative, one that will carry us from the fragmented tribes of the Mongolian steppes to the consolidated might of the Mongol Empire. In the tales of these tribes, we find the echoes of our own struggles for identity and cohesion, our own search for leadership that can navigate the treacherous terrain of human ambition and rivalry.

The journey has only just begun. Ahead lies the saga of Genghis Khan and his unification of the Mongol people, a tale of strategy, conquest, and the indomitable will of one man to change the world. Through this historical lens, we may yet glean insights into the nature of power, leadership, and the eternal quest for legacy that drives the human spirit.

The Unification of the Mongol Tribes

EMBARKING ON THE MONUMENTAL journey of uniting the disparate Mongol tribes, one must fathom the monumental undertaking Genghis Khan confronted. This narrative shall traverse the intricate web of strategies and battles that sculpted the tribes into a single, formidable force under his indomitable leadership.

Imagine, if you will, a leader who gazes upon the vast expanse of the steppe, not as a series of isolated lands but as a potential empire united under a single banner. That was the vision that fueled Temujin's ambition, an ambition that required not only courage and cunning but also an intimate knowledge of Mongol customs, alliances, and the art of war.

Before the unification could commence, prerequisites demanded attention. These were not mere tangible materials, but rather, intangible assets like loyalty, respect, and strategic acumen. Also required was an unparalleled mastery of horsemanship and combat, a deep understanding of the Mongolian landscape, and the ability to forge alliances with or vanquish rival tribes.

The overview of this monumental task began with the consolidation of his own tribe and extended to forging alliances through marriage, diplomacy, and sometimes through raw displays of power. Next, he would systematically challenge and defeat rival tribes, drawing their warriors into his own ranks and integrating their customs and tactics into a diverse yet unified military force.

Detailing this process reveals the genius of Genghis Khan's approach. He began by securing his position within his family tribe, the Borjigin, through a combination of traditional leadership and innovative tactics. He recognized the importance of alliances, and through marriage to Borte, he gained the support of the Khereid tribe. His wife's abduction by the Merkit tribe provided the impetus for a campaign that not only reclaimed his spouse but also established his prowess as a military leader.

But how did he ensure the loyalty of the tribes he conquered? One might ponder this while considering the innovative laws he implemented, known as the Yassa, which codified behavior and ensured a measure of justice and order previously unseen on the steppe.

Would you not agree that the ability to inspire and maintain loyalty is the mark of a true leader? Genghis Khan offered captured warriors a place in his ranks, a choice that often proved more appealing than the prospect of death or return to a defeated tribe. He also had a unique approach to leadership, promoting individuals based on merit and loyalty rather than tribal affiliation or nobility.

There are tips to be gleaned from his methods—like the utility of mercy as a tool for winning hearts and minds, and the wisdom of adopting and adapting the best practices of those you defeat. He warned against complacency and underestimating one's enemies, a lesson many would learn too late as they faced him in battle.

The validation of Genghis Khan's efforts was in the loyalty and effectiveness of his army, the swiftness of his conquests, and the establishment of a legal system that transcended tribal laws. His unification of the Mongol tribes was not a fleeting occurrence but the foundation of what would become one of the largest empires in history.

Yet, one must acknowledge that not all efforts met with success. There were tribes that resisted, alliances that faltered, and internal strife that threatened to unravel the fabric of his burgeoning empire. Within these challenges, however, lay the opportunity for troubleshooting—an opportunity to adapt and overcome, traits that Genghis Khan possessed in abundance.

Thus, the story of the unification under Genghis Khan is not a mere recounting of victories and defeats but an intricate dance of strategy, diplomacy, and indomitable will. It is a testament to the power of a clear vision and the relentless pursuit of that vision against all odds.

As we delve deeper into the annals of history, let us not merely observe the tactical genius of Genghis Khan but also reflect upon the enduring lessons his journey offers. Let us embrace the spirit of the steppe that breathes life into these pages, offering insights into leadership, unity, and the relentless pursuit of greatness.

The Mongol War Machine

THROUGHOUT MILITARY history, few armies have struck as much fear and awe as the Mongol hordes led by the legendary Genghis Khan. These warriors emerged from the steppes of Central Asia, not just as conquerors, but as innovators of warfare. This exploration delves into the martial excellence of the Mongol Empire, dissecting the military tactics and innovations that made this army an unstoppable force that reshaped the world.

The Mongol military machine was a marvel of its time, predicated on the combination of speed, discipline, and a flexible approach to warfare that allowed it to adapt and overcome the diverse challenges posed by the varied terrain and enemies it encountered. At the heart of the Mongol army's success was its revolutionary approach to combat, an approach that enabled a relatively small force to conquer vast territories, outmaneuvering and outthinking larger, more established armies.

The primary evidence of the Mongol army's prowess lies in its unparalleled mastery of the composite bow and horsemanship. The Mongols were trained from a young age to shoot with deadly accuracy while mounted, a skill that made them formidable in battle. This fearsome combination allowed the Mongols to rain arrows upon their enemies with a rapidity and precision that was unmatched. Their bows, made from layers of horn and sinew, were engineered to deliver powerful shots over great distances, even when the horse was in full gallop.

But to truly understand the might of the Mongol army, one must look beyond their weaponry and examine their tactics. The Mongols employed a sophisticated system of signals, using flags and drums to communicate across the battlefield, coordinating their movements with an efficiency that left little room for error. Their intelligence network, comprised of extensive scouting and the use of spies, provided vital information regarding the terrain, enemy positions, and movements. This intelligence allowed them to execute strategic maneuvers like the feigned retreat, a tactic that lured opponents into traps where the Mongols could then encircle and decimate them.

Yet, this narrative would be incomplete without acknowledging the counter-evidence that suggests the Mongol army's strength was sometimes exaggerated by the very people they conquered. Fearful accounts may have amplified the Mongols' ferocity and strategic genius to justify their own failures. Some historians propose that factors like internal strife, disease, and sheer luck played significant roles in the Mongol conquests.

In rebuttal, while external factors undoubtedly influenced the outcomes of certain battles, the consistent success of the Mongol army across varied campaigns and against diverse opponents speaks to an inherent military effectiveness. The Mongols adapted their tactics to siege warfare when conquering cities, employing engineers and utilizing captured enemies to build and operate siege engines. Their adaptability in warfare is a testament to their versatility and innovation, rather than mere chance or the weakness of their adversaries.

Adding to this, the Mongol army's logistical support system was revolutionary. They traveled with a mobile infrastructure that included a network of supply points and herds of animals, ensuring that their warriors were well-provisioned and could maintain their stamina over long campaigns. This logistical acumen allowed them to sustain campaigns far from their homeland, a feat few armies could match.

The conclusion that emerges from this analysis is clear: the Mongol military machine was a product of meticulous planning, exceptional training, and innovative tactics. The very essence of their military dominance was rooted in a culture that valued strength, resilience, and the ability to adapt to any challenge. The Mongol army was not just a force of destruction but a crucible of innovation that forever altered the landscape of warfare.

As the sun set on the vast steppe, the echoes of Mongol hooves faded into history, leaving behind a legacy of military ingenuity. The Mongol Empire may have dissolved with time, yet the strategies and tactics developed by this nomadic army continue to inspire and influence modern military thought. Who can gaze upon the vastness of their conquests without a sense of wonder at the sheer audacity and brilliance of their war machine? In the end, the Mongol army's legacy is a testament to the power of innovation and strategy in the art of war.

Code of Laws: The Yassa

IN THE VAST EXPANSE of the Mongol Empire, as it stretched from the Pacific to the heart of Europe, a singular legal code, known as the Yassa, served as the backbone of Genghis Khan's dominion. This code not only structured Mongol society but also played a pivotal role in their military conquests. Grasping the intricacies of this code necessitates an understanding of the specific terms that underpin it, much like knowing the rules of a game before setting out to play.

Readers will embark on a journey through the Yassa, uncovering its components and their impacts. To navigate this exploration effectively, one must first become familiar with a roster of terms that are vital to a comprehensive understanding of this legal framework.

At the forefront of our exploration stands the Yassa itself, followed by other crucial terms such as 'Tumen', 'Noyan', 'Kurultai', 'Anda', and 'Arban'. Each of these words, while perhaps unfamiliar at first, unlocks a segment of the Mongol world that Genghis Khan meticulously constructed.

The Yassa, translated as "order" or "decree," was the overarching legal code established by Genghis Khan. Far more than a mere collection of laws, the Yassa was a cultural adhesive that bound the diverse peoples of the Mongol Empire together under a unified set of principles and regulations. At its core, the Yassa fostered a sense of order and discipline that was crucial for the cohesion and efficiency of the Mongol military forces.

A 'Tumen' was a military unit consisting of 10,000 warriors, a number not arbitrary but deeply rooted in the administrative genius of the Mongols, which allowed for a systematic and scalable approach to organizing their vast army. The 'Noyan', a title given to high-ranking military commanders, were entrusted with leading these units, imbuing them with the authority to enforce the Yassa among their ranks.

The 'Kurultai', an assembly of Mongol chiefs, was integral to the political life of the Empire. It was here that laws were proclaimed, strategies were formulated, and leaders, including the Great Khan himself, were elected. The processes and outcomes of the Kurultai were bound by the principles of the Yassa, ensuring that even the highest echelons of Mongol leadership were subject to the rule of law.

'Anda', meaning blood brother or sworn friend, denotes a bond between individuals that transcended biological kinship, a connection forged through oath and ritual that the Yassa held in high esteem. This concept was essential in maintaining the loyalty and unity among the Mongol ranks, as bonds of 'anda' often translated into unwavering military alliances.

An 'Arban' referred to a group of ten soldiers, the smallest unit in the Mongol military hierarchy. The solidarity and effectiveness of each arban were critical to the success of larger units, and by extension, the entire Mongol army. The Yassa governed the conduct within these groups, ensuring that every soldier adhered to the same discipline and order that characterized the Mongol military ethos.

The real-world implications of these terms are profound. Consider the 'tumen', a concept that mirrors modern military organization with its regiments and divisions, showcasing the Mongols' advanced understanding of structured command. The 'noyan' reflects the role of modern-day generals, while the 'kurultai' can be seen as an early form of a parliamentary or council system. The 'anda' is akin to the bonds found in fraternal orders or among soldiers in contemporary armies who share a brotherhood forged in the crucible of shared experiences. Lastly, the 'arban' evokes the modern military squad, the fundamental building block of larger forces.

Genghis Khan's Yassa was thus not merely a legal code but a reflection of a deeply ingrained military and social philosophy. It was this philosophy that allowed the Mongols to cultivate loyalty and maintain order across the vast distances and diverse cultures of their empire. Through the Yassa, the Mongol Empire was able to function as a cohesive and formidable entity, despite the challenges posed by its size and diversity.

To the casual observer, the Yassa might seem an arcane relic of a bygone era. Yet, to those who look closely, it reveals itself as a testament to the Mongol Empire's sophisticated approach to governance and military organization. The code's influence on the success of the Mongols cannot be overstated; it was the sinew that connected the limbs of the empire, the drumbeat to which the hooves of their horses marched.

From the ger camps of the steppes to the palaces in Karakorum, the Yassa was the unseen hand guiding the Mongol world. Through it, Genghis Khan forged an empire that, though it has crumbled into the sands of time, still whispers to us about the power of law and order in creating and maintaining a society. The Yassa was not just a list of do's and don'ts; it was the DNA of the Mongol Empire, a code that breathed life into the vision of one of history's most formidable leaders.

Expansion Under Genghis Khan

Conquest of the Xi Xia and Jin Dynasties

Throughout history, few empires have conjured images of awe and grandeur as does the Mongol Empire. Its rise to power not only reshaped the political landscape of Asia but also left an indelible mark on the world. As we delve into the Mongols' initial forays into empire-building, we recount their campaigns against the Xi Xia and Jin dynasties, fierce struggles that heralded the dawn of their expansion.

The origins of the Mongol Empire's military might can be traced back to the unification of the Mongol tribes under the iron-willed leadership of Temujin, who would later be known as Genghis Khan. This inception point marked a paradigm shift in the steppes of Central Asia; the year 1206 witnessed the birth of a force that would sweep across the continent.

Chronicle these milestones: the relentless siege of the Xi Xia capital in 1209, the grueling campaign against the Jin dynasty beginning in 1211, and the pivotal battle of Yehuling in 1213. Each a testament to the Mongols' growing prowess. Enhance the saga with images of ancient battle maps, depicting the strategic brilliance of the Mongol generals.

As the narrative unfolds, one must consider the diversity within the Mongol ranks. They assimilated warriors from conquered territories, integrating disparate military traditions into their own. This fusion of cultures under the banner of the Mongol Empire contributed to their innovative tactics and adaptability in warfare.

Reflect on the modern interpretations of these conquests. Historians and scholars decipher the Mongol military strategies, seeking to understand how a nomadic people could subjugate sedentary empires. The lessons drawn from these analyses continue to influence modern military thought.

Yet, no historical recount is without its controversies. The conquests brought immense suffering to the subjugated peoples, and the moral implications of the Mongol expansion remain a topic of heated debate. The siege of the Xi Xia, for example, culminated in a massacre that some modern scholars label as genocide.

Can you imagine the unyielding determination of the Mongol horde as they laid waste to the Xi Xia's defenses? Picture the Jin soldiers, outnumbered and outmaneuvered, facing the inexorable tide of horsemen on the horizon. The thunder of hooves, the clash of steel, the cries of the fallen - these were the harbingers of a new era.

It was in these crucibles of conflict that the Mongol Empire began to forge its legacy. With each victory, Genghis Khan's vision of a vast dominion stretching from the Pacific to the Caspian Sea crept closer to reality. The conquests of the Xi Xia and Jin dynasties were but the first steps in what would become one of the most extraordinary tales of expansion in human history.

Yet, amidst the recounting of sieges and battles, one must pause and reflect. What was the cost of such relentless conquest? What legacy, wrought from the swords and arrows of the Mongol warriors, endures in the lands they once dominated?

In the end, the Mongol campaigns against Xi Xia and Jin represent more than just military triumphs. They signify the transformation of the Mongol identity from scattered tribes to a unified force that challenged the very notion of what an empire could be. Through their conquests, the Mongols not only carved out an empire but also sowed the seeds for the cultural and economic exchanges along the Silk Road that would shape the world for centuries to come.

The Mongol Empire, with its complex history of conquest and integration, continues to captivate the imagination. Its story serves as a stark reminder of the transient nature of power and the enduring impact of human ambition. And so, we continue to study, to learn, and to remember.

Invasion of Central Asia

THE MONGOL EMPIRE, with its fierce warriors and even more formidable reputation, turned its gaze upon Central Asia. What lay ahead was a campaign that would not only expand their empire but also intertwine destinies across a vast and varied landscape. But what catalyzed this colossal movement of Mongol forces into the heartland of Eurasia?

Historians point to the desire for riches, resources, and strategic depth as primary motivations. Central Asia, with its prosperous cities and well-established trade routes, presented an irresistible lure for an empire in expansionist mode. Yet, the Mongol approach was not merely one of brute force; it was nuanced, strategic, and, at times, diplomatically shrewd.

The problem lay in the complex nature of Central Asian politics. The Khwarezmian Empire, a major power in the region, initially offered a chance for peaceful relations. But when a Mongol trade caravan and then an embassy were massacred, the Mongols responded with a full-scale invasion. The sheer scale of the resulting devastation was unprecedented, and the consequences were far-reaching.

One could ask, what if the Mongols had chosen diplomacy over destruction? The death toll would have been vastly reduced, and the social fabric of the region might have remained intact. Instead, the Mongol incursions left a trail of razed cities from Bukhara to Samarkand, and the very name of Genghis Khan became synonymous with merciless conquest.

The solution, it seemed, was to establish a new order in Central Asia—one that would ensure stability and prosperity under Mongol rule. Genghis Khan and his successors aimed to weave the conquered lands into their empire's fabric through a combination of military might and administrative acumen.

Implementing this vision required a sophisticated blend of tolerance and control. The Mongols allowed religious freedom and trade to flourish, yet they imposed a strict regime that demanded loyalty and tribute. They rebuilt cities and patronized the arts and sciences, fostering what would become a renaissance of culture and intellect in the Ilkhanate and beyond.

The outcome of these policies was a paradoxical mix of cultural exchange and economic growth, juxtaposed against a backdrop of societal trauma and population displacement. The Silk Road thrived as never before, bringing wealth and knowledge to the Mongol Empire, but at a cost that historians still debate today.

Some suggest alternative solutions might have mitigated the suffering. Could a more merciful approach have preserved the region's integrity while still achieving the Mongol's strategic goals? Unfortunately, the terror instilled by the Mongols was also a calculated tactic to suppress resistance, making this question more complex than it seems.

The Mongol invasions of Central Asia thus became a turning point in history, a moment when the destiny of nations was rewritten with arrow and sword. The cultural and economic impacts of these events are still felt today, echoes of a time when a single empire's ambition reshaped the world.

In the chapters of history, the Mongol incursions into Central Asia are not merely a footnote. They are a reminder of how the tides of conquest can alter the course of human civilization. As the dust settled on the ravaged steppes and cities began to rise from the ashes, a new era dawned—an era marked by the mingling of cultures, the exchange of ideas, and the indomitable spirit of humanity to rebuild and endure amidst the greatest of adversities.

In the grand tapestry of the Mongol Empire's history, the invasion of Central Asia is a vivid and compelling narrative. It speaks of ambition, destruction, resilience, and the complex interplay of power and culture. It is a story that merits deep reflection, for it holds lessons about the nature of empires and the enduring consequences of their actions. What legacy, then, did the Mongols leave in the sands and cities of Central Asia? A legacy carved by the sword, yes, but also by the pen and the caravan trail—a legacy that continues to shape the world in ways both seen and unseen.

The Battle of Kalka River

IN THE EARLY 13TH CENTURY, the Mongol Empire, under the rule of Genghis Khan, embarked on a series of relentless conquests that would reshape the world. The swift currents of the Kalka River, flowing through what is now Ukraine, were soon to witness a pivotal moment in the Mongol expansion—a moment that would exemplify the tactical genius and ruthless efficiency of the Mongol military machine.

As dawn stretched its fingers over the vast steppe, the banks of the Kalka River were shrouded in a tense silence. The year was 1223, and the stage was set for a confrontation that would sear itself into the annals of military history. Here, the Mongol forces, led by the shrewd generals Subutai and Jebe, stood on the brink of a battle against a coalition of Rus' principalities, commanded by Mstislav the Bold of Galicia and Mstislav III of Kiev.

The Rus', a proud collection of warrior elites, held dominion over a fragmented territory. Their principalities, fiercely independent but united in the face of a common enemy, had been alerted to the Mongol threat by the devastation wrought in neighboring lands. The challenge was clear and present: repel the Mongols or be swept away by their unrelenting tide.

The Mongols, renowned for their horse archery and mobility, brought to the field a host of ingenious strategies that had already brought empires to their knees. Subutai and Jebe, veterans of numerous campaigns, devised a plan that would leverage their strengths in mobility and deception. By feigning a retreat, they lured the Rus' into a chase, stretching their forces thin over several days. The Mongols' approach was a masterful manipulation of psychology and terrain.

After the grueling pursuit, the Mongols turned to face their now weary and disorganized adversaries. With a sudden and ferocious onslaught, they unleashed their full might upon the unsuspecting Rus' forces. The Rus', caught in a pincer movement, were trapped between the jaws of the Mongol war machine.

The carnage that unfolded was swift and merciless. The Rus' were decimated, their numbers cut down like wheat before the scythe. The Mongols, with their composite bows and expert horsemanship, dominated the battlefield, exemplifying the lethal synthesis of speed and firepower.

The aftermath of the battle was harrowing. The Rus' suffered staggering losses, with thousands slain or captured. The Mongols, meanwhile, emerged with minimal casualties, their reputation as invincible warriors further cemented. The significance of this victory was manifold: not only had the Mongols devastated a formidable foe, but they had also sown terror deep into the heart of Europe.

As historians, we must reflect on this moment with both awe and dismay. The Mongols' military prowess is undeniable, but the human cost of their victories paints a somber picture. Could the Rus' have employed a different strategy to avert disaster? Would a more cautious approach have spared lives and staved off defeat? These questions linger, inviting contemplation on the nature of warfare and the decisions that lead to triumph or tragedy.

The Battle of Kalka River was not simply an isolated skirmish; it was a harbinger of the Mongol Empire's far-reaching ambitions. By defeating the Rus', the Mongols demonstrated their capability to extend their influence far beyond the familiar steppes of Central Asia. They stood on the precipice of a new era, one where their dominion would touch every corner of the known world.

One might ponder, as the sun set on the blood-soaked fields near the Kalka River, what thoughts occupied the minds of Subutai and Jebe. Did they foresee the ripple effects of their victory, how it would echo through the corridors of time, influencing tactics and the art of war for generations to come?

The Battle of Kalka River remains a testament to the indomitable spirit of the Mongol warriors and a grim reminder of the devastation wrought in the pursuit of empire. As we turn the page on this chapter of history, we are left to muse on the cycles of conquest and the enduring legacy of empires built by sword and bow. What lessons, then, can we glean from the ashes of battle, and how do they shape our understanding of the past and our vision for the future?

Western Xia and the Khwarezm Empire

THE SANDS OF THE GOBI Desert and the fertile valleys of Central Asia bore witness to the relentless march of the Mongol Empire, an unstoppable force that left a profound mark on the course of history. Two of the most significant conquests undertaken by the Mongols were against the Western Xia and the Khwarezm Empire. These campaigns not only demonstrated the Mongols' military prowess but also their strategic acumen in dealing with vastly different adversaries.

The purpose of drawing a comparison between these two conquests is to shed light on the Mongolian methods of warfare and governance, and to understand how these approaches dictated the fate of the empires that stood in their path. By examining these historical events side by side, we gain a deeper insight into the Mongol Empire's expansion and its long-lasting effects on world history.

Our analysis hinges on several criteria: the strategic and tactical practices employed by the Mongols, the political context surrounding each invasion, the military technologies in use, and the aftermath of these conquests, including the administrative policies that followed.

Both the Western Xia and the Khwarezm Empire faced a similar foe in the Mongols, yet the outcomes of their encounters bore striking differences rooted in how each empire engaged with the Mongol threat. The Western Xia, a Tangut Buddhist kingdom, had a complex relationship with the Mongols, involving a plethura of alliances and betrayals. The Khwarezm Empire, with its Persian-Islamic culture, was a rising power that controlled a vast territory stretching from the Amu Darya to the Persian Gulf.

The Mongols employed similar tactics in their campaigns against both empires. Their approach to warfare was marked by extraordinary mobility, psychological warfare, and the strategic use of terror. The Mongol army, adept in horseback archery and rapid maneuvers, could strike with precision and vanish just as quickly, sapping the enemy's will to fight.

However, the contrast lies in how each empire responded. The Western Xia, having experienced intermittent conflicts and periods of uneasy peace with the Mongols, attempted to appease Genghis Khan through tribute and support in his campaigns against other rivals. The Khwarezm Empire, on the other hand, sealed its fate with a series of diplomatic blunders, culminating in the murder of Mongol envoys—a grave insult that Genghis Khan could not ignore.

The Mongol invasion of the Western Xia was marked by sieges and battles that tested the limits of Mongol ingenuity. With fortified cities and a harsh landscape to their advantage, the Western Xia resisted fiercely. Yet, the Mongols adapted, employing siege engines and diversifying tactics to overcome these obstacles.

In stark contrast, the Mongols faced the Khwarezm Empire with an unbridled fury, sparked by the affront to their honor. The resulting campaign was one of utter devastation, with cities like Bukhara and Samarkand facing wholesale slaughter and destruction. The Mongols not only sought victory but also aimed to make an example of the Khwarezm Empire, broadcasting a clear message to any who would dare oppose them.

The aftermath of these conquests differed as well. In Western Xia, the Mongols eventually installed a puppet ruler before fully annexing the territory, whereas in the Khwarezm Empire, the Mongols dismantled the state structure, leaving a power vacuum that would shape the political landscape for years to come.

These campaigns speak volumes about the Mongol approach to empire-building. Their ability to integrate conquered peoples, tolerance for different cultures, and pragmatic governance contrasted with their reputation for brutality and destruction. The Mongols were not mere conquerors; they were shapers of the world order, leaving behind a legacy of trade, cultural exchange, and even the dissemination of technologies.

What can contemporary readers learn from these historical episodes? The Mongol Empire's expansion serves as a reminder of the dual nature of power—the capacity for both creation and annihilation. It invites us to ponder the paradox of empires, which can simultaneously advance civilization and deliver untold suffering.

As the dust settled over the ruins of once-great cities and the silence of the steppes returned, one might wonder if the Mongol leaders contemplated the full scope of their actions. Did they envision a world united under their rule, or were they driven purely by the desire for conquest and retribution? The echoes of their decisions continue to resonate, challenging us to reflect on the complex tapestry of human ambition and the relentless tide of history that shapes our existence.

Genghis Khan's Legacy

THE INDELIBLE MARK of Genghis Khan's empire is etched not only in the vast stretches of conquered lands but also in the multifaceted legacies that continue to influence our global fabric. His conquests transcended mere territorial expansion, seeding transformative effects that have rippled through time, touching upon governance, culture, trade, and the very way wars are waged.

In the forthcoming pages, we shall embark on a journey to unravel these legacies, to understand the profound and lasting impacts of Genghis Khan's empire on the stage of world history. This exploration is crucial, for it allows us to perceive the Mongol Empire not just as a historical phenomenon but as a shaping force whose influence is still felt in contemporary times.

The Pax Mongolica and Global Trade

Under the widespread peace enforced by Mongol rule, known as the Pax Mongolica, an unprecedented surge in trade and economic growth occurred. The Mongol Empire connected and secured trade routes across Asia and Europe, facilitating a flourishing exchange of goods, ideas, and technologies.

Evidence of the Pax Mongolica's impact on trade is found in the historical accounts of travelers such as Marco Polo, whose travels might not have been possible without the relative security provided by the Mongol governance. The flow of silk, spices, and precious metals not only enriched merchants but also funded cultural and urban developments across continents.

Practical applications of the Pax Mongolica are seen in modern efforts to establish international trade agreements that aim to replicate the stability and prosperity that was once achieved under the Mongol Empire. Today's globalization owes a conceptual debt to the Mongol-induced connectivity of diverse cultures and economies.

The Yassa: Codification of Laws and Governance

The Yassa, Genghis Khan's codification of laws, laid the foundation for a unified legal framework that governed the diverse peoples of his empire. This legal system was instrumental in maintaining order and justice, and it helped to integrate the various ethnic groups under Mongol rule.

The Yassa's principles, emphasizing loyalty, military discipline, and punishment for thievery and adultery, are echoed in modern legal systems that value order and societal norms. The Mongol's approach to governance, with its blend of strictness and pragmatism, offers a historical precedent for contemporary legal reforms that seek a balance between discipline and fairness.

Military Innovations and Tactics

Genghis Khan revolutionized warfare with his use of military intelligence, psychological warfare, and innovative tactics. The Mongol military's reliance on swift horseback archers, efficient communication systems, and the strategic use of fear left a lasting imprint on the art of war.

The echoes of Mongol military ingenuity resonate in today's doctrines that value speed, flexibility, and psychological operations. Modern militaries study the Mongol campaigns to glean insights into unconventional warfare and rapid deployment forces.

Cultural and Religious Tolerance

Remarkably, the Mongol Empire was known for its cultural and religious tolerance. Genghis Khan allowed his subjects to practice their religions and customs freely, fostering a milieu of coexistence.

This legacy is a testament to the potential for diverse societies to thrive under a strict law of mutual respect and is reflected in modern policies that promote multiculturalism nerd religious freedom.

Demographic Changes and Genetic Legacy

The Mongol conquests brought about significant demographic shifts through population displacement, intermarriage, and the integration of various ethnic groups. Genetic studies suggest that

Genghis Khan's lineage is present in a considerable proportion of men in the territories once under Mongol control, indicating a widespread genetic legacy.

These findings have profound implications for our understanding of human migration patterns and genetic diversity. They highlight how historical events can shape the genetic makeup of populations over centuries.

The Silk Road and Cultural Exchange

The revitalization of the Silk Road under Mongol rule facilitated an unprecedented cultural and intellectual exchange. Knowledge, art, and religious beliefs traversed these routes alongside merchants and envoys, contributing to the diffusion of innovations such as paper money, gunpowder, and medical knowledge.

The Silk Road's historical role as a conduit for cultural exchange serves as an inspiration for contemporary initiatives that seek to foster international collaboration and the sharing of knowledge across borders.

As we traverse from one legacy to the next, the image of Genghis Khan's empire becomes multifaceted, revealing a complex tapestry woven from the threads of conquest, innovation, and tolerance. Each page turned is a step deeper into the understanding of how a single ruler's vision could reshape the world in ways that would resonate through the ages.

What lessons can we draw from the intricate mosaic of the Mongol Empire's influence? Does the blueprint of Genghis Khan's rule offer insights into the art of leadership and the wielding of power? Let us ponder these questions, for they are as relevant today as they were in the time of the great khan.

The legacy of Genghis Khan, much like the steppes that once echoed with the thunder of Mongol horses, is vast and enduring. As we conclude this segment of our exploration, we recognize that the reverberations of the Mongol Empire's impact are not confined to history books; they are alive, shaping the contours of our modern world in subtle but powerful ways.

The Reign of the Khans

Ogedei Khan: The Empire's Architect

In the vast, rolling steppes of Mongolia, where the sky kisses the earth at a horizon that stretches into infinity, a great gathering stirred the dust of the plains. It was the year 1229, and the Mongol chieftains, their faces etched with the lines of countless battles and the wisdom of nomadic life, converged upon the revered and feared center of their burgeoning empire. Amid the throng of warriors and horses, one figure commanded an air of quiet authority, his presence as solid and unassuming as the land from which he rose. This was Ogedei, son of Genghis Khan, the man upon whose shoulders lay the colossal task of erecting an empire that would rewrite the annals of history.

The scene at this kurultai, a grand council of Mongol leaders, was charged with the palpable tension of a pivotal moment in time. Ogedei, though not as physically imposing as his legendary father, possessed a keen intellect and a demeanor that inspired both loyalty and discipline. His eyes, dark and probing, seemed to hold the vastness of the steppe itself, and in their depths swirled the dreams and fears of the Mongol people.

As the council unfolded, Ogedei's voice cut through the air with the precision of an arrow, his words shaping the future with each sentence. His vision for the empire was not solely built on conquest and the spoils of war but on the foundations of administration and law. Here was an empire that would not merely vanquish but would govern, bringing disparate peoples under the yoke of a Pax Mongolica.

Could it be that this man, viewed by some as merely a fortunate son, was, in fact, a master architect of power? The onlookers, with their breath held tight in their chests, dared not blink, for history was being written with each decree Ogedei issued.

In the annals of history, Ogedei Khan is perhaps overshadowed by the towering figure of his father, Genghis Khan, and the notorious reputation of his brother, the wild and tempestuous Chagatai. Yet, it was Ogedei who would steer the ship of the Mongol Empire through the treacherous waters of succession, expansion, and governance. His reign, though not free from the intoxicating lure of conquest, marked a turning point in the empire's trajectory, from a horde of skilled warriors to a more sophisticated geopolitical entity.

But who was this man, really? What drove him, and how did he perceive the weight of an empire upon his shoulders? Was he merely a placeholder, a caretaker of his father's legacy, or was he the true consolidator of the Mongol conquests?

Picture Ogedei, sitting in his ger, the traditional felt tent of the Mongols, his fingers tracing the lines of a map that sprawled across a low wooden table. The map was a living thing, its boundaries expanding and contracting with each campaign, each alliance, each act of rebellion. Ogedei's mind, ever calculating, was a cauldron of strategy, diplomacy, and foresight.

The empire he inherited was vast, stretching from the Sea of Japan to the heart of Europe, a realm of endless possibilities and innumerable challenges. What universal truths can we glean from Ogedei's story? Is it the inexorable march of destiny that shapes the world, or the deliberate strokes of a leader's brush upon the canvas of history? And what wisdom does his tale hold for us, the modern readers, as we navigate the complex web of our own societal structures?

His story is not just a chronicle of conquests and decrees but a narrative of human ambition, frailty, and the ceaseless quest for order in a world of chaos. Through the lens of his life, may we come to understand the delicate balance between power and governance, between the sword and the scroll.

Mongke Khan: Administrative Reforms

IN THE WAKE OF OGEDEI Khan's tenure as the ruler of the Mongol Empire, the realm found itself at a crossroads. The whispering winds of the steppe carried murmurs of unrest, and the empire's vastness began to strain under the weight of its own expanse. Enter Mongke Khan, the grandson of Genghis Khan, who ascended to the throne in 1251 with a keen understanding that the sprawling empire required more than the might of warriors to sustain its glory. He was faced with a significant issue: the administrative apparatus of the empire was ill-equipped to handle its burgeoning complexity and diversity.

The primary challenge lay in the patchwork of territories, each with its own customs and systems of governance, now unified under the Mongol banner. The lack of standardized administration threatened the very cohesion of the empire, potentially leading to inefficiency, corruption, and rebellion. The consequences of ignoring this ticking time bomb of administrative dissonance were dire: the empire risked fragmenting into feuding fiefdoms, squandering the unity painstakingly forged by Mongke's forefathers.

Mongke Khan's solution to this burgeoning crisis was as pragmatic as it was visionary. He proposed a sweeping reform of the empire's administrative machinery, a reorganization that would standardize procedures and enforce accountability. At the heart of these reforms was the introduction of a merit-based bureaucracy, drawing from both Mongol and non-Mongol talent, ensuring that the most capable individuals governed the localities entrusted to them.

The first step Mongke took was a thorough census across the empire. A census, you might wonder? Indeed, a tool as mundane as a census provided the data necessary to understand the empire's vast resources and diverse populations. It was a mammoth task, one that required meticulous planning and execution. The census takers, often literate scribes from different ethnic backgrounds, ventured into every corner of the empire, documenting the populace, wealth, and resources available.

This census laid the groundwork for what would become a more equitable taxation system, replacing the arbitrary levies with a standardized tax code. With a clearer picture of the empire's demographics and wealth, Mongke was able to allocate resources more efficiently and assess the empire's military and economic capabilities with unprecedented precision.

But what were the outcomes of these audacious reforms? The evidence lay in the relative peace and stability that followed. The streamlined bureaucracy fostered an environment where trade flourished, and the Silk Road, that artery of cultural and economic exchange, thrived under the protective gaze of the Mongols. The empire, once teetering on the edge of internal discord, found a new sense of purpose and unity.

Of course, there were alternative solutions proposed by Mongke's advisors—some suggested further military campaigns to distract from internal issues, while others believed in maintaining the status quo. However, Mongke, with his foresight and dedication to the long-term prosperity of his empire, knew that these were mere stopgaps, temporary measures that would not address the root of the problem.

His reforms were not without their detractors, and implementing such widespread change was akin to steering a colossal ship against a relentless tide. Resistance came from traditionalist elements within the Mongol elite who viewed the influx of foreign administrators with suspicion. Yet, Mongke's resolute leadership and the tangible benefits of his policies gradually won over the skeptics.

Visualize, if you will, the bustling markets from Samarkand to Karakorum, teeming with goods from around the known world, a testament to the success of Mongke Khan's reforms. Imagine the scribes, diligently recording transactions and taxes, a reflection of the newfound order within the empire. Can you not perceive the silent, yet profound strength in these scenes of daily life?

Mongke Khan's legacy is not merely in the grandeur of his military campaigns or the expanse of the territories under his rule, but in the lasting administrative structures he established. These reforms shaped the Mongol Empire into a more cohesive and effective entity, one capable of enduring the tests of time far beyond the reign of one man.

Through the delicate interplay of power and governance, Mongke Khan understood that the true strength of an empire lay not only in its ability to conquer but also in its capacity to administer, to adapt, and to unify.

Kublai Khan: A New Horizon

NEXT, KUBLAI KHAN EMERGED as a beacon of change. His reign was the dawning of a new horizon, an era where the might of the Mongol Empire would be channeled not solely through the strength of its horses and the sharpness of its arrows, but through the grandeur of its cultural and economic transformations.

The tale begins with Kublai, grandson of Genghis Khan and brother to Mongke Khan, who ascended to the throne in 1260. His inheritance was an empire at the zenith of its power yet teetering on the precipice of a new age that demanded innovation over invasion, diplomacy over destruction.

The Yuan Dynasty, Kublai Khan's magnum opus, marked the inception point of his legacy. It was not merely the continuation of Mongol rule; it was a metamorphosis, a synthesis of the nomadic Mongol heritage with the sedentary civilizations it now encompassed. Kublai's vision was to shepherd these disparate cultures into a single, harmonious whole, under the aegis of his enlightened governance.

The chronology of Kublai's milestones is a testament to his multifaceted leadership. He began by relocating the capital from Karakorum to Dadu, present-day Beijing, a move symbolic of the shift from the steppes to the settled lands of China. The city itself was transformed into a cosmopolitan hub, with palaces, observatories, and gardens that reflected the Khan's broad tastes and openness to diverse influences.

The grandeur of Dadu was complemented by the construction of the legendary summer capital, Xanadu. Here, poets and artists found inspiration, and the confluence of Mongol and Chinese aesthetics gave birth to a new architectural style. As you let your imagination wander through the marble terraces and silk-draped pavilions of Xanadu, can you feel the pulse of an empire in the throes of cultural renaissance?

Kublai's reign was marked by the establishment of a centralized bureaucracy that drew from the talents of Chinese, Persians, and Europeans alike. The introduction of paper currency revolutionized the economy, facilitating trade and commerce across the vastness of the empire. Such an economic innovation begs the question: how did Kublai Khan foresee the power of this intangible currency, a concept so far removed from the tangible wealth of gold and silver?

The construction of the Grand Canal, an engineering marvel that stitched the empire together, was another of Kublai's significant achievements. It enabled the efficient movement of grain and resources, ensuring the stability and prosperity of his realm.

One must not forget Kublai's patronage of arts and sciences. The Polos, a family of Venetian merchants led by the famed Marco Polo, were among those drawn to Kublai's court, bringing with them knowledge and stories from the far reaches of the world. The Khan's interest in diverse religions and philosophies further exemplified his expansive view of empire, one that embraced a multitude of beliefs and ideas.

However, Kublai's rule was not without its challenges. The difficult conquest of the Southern Song dynasty, the resistance from traditional Mongol elites, and natural disasters tested the resilience of his administration. Yet, it is in the crucible of these adversities that Kublai's ingenuity and adaptability shone brightest.

As the years progressed, the Yuan Dynasty faced internal strife and external pressures, culminating in its eventual decline. Yet, the cultural and economic innovations of Kublai Khan's reign endured, leaving an indelible imprint on the fabric of Chinese history. His was a legacy characterized by the bold fusion of cultures, the daring implementation of economic reforms, and the audacious reimagining of what a Mongol empire could be.

In modern interpretations, Kublai Khan is often seen as a ruler who bridged East and West, a precursor to the global interconnectedness we experience today. His reign is a reminder that the strength of an empire lies as much in its cultural achievements and economic foresight as it does in its military might.

Thus, the horizon that Kublai Khan gazed upon was not merely the edge of his empire's vast lands, but the unfolding future of cultural synthesis, economic innovation, and enduring legacy. As we reflect upon his triumphs and tribulations, let us ask ourselves: what horizons are we setting our sights upon, and how will the legacies we leave behind shape the future?

The Khanates: Division of an Empire

IN THE WAKE OF KUBLAI Khan's grand vision, the vast Mongol Empire, once a contiguous dominion under the singular rule of Genghis Khan's iron will, began to fracture like parched earth under a relentless sun. The once unified entity splintered into a quartet of distinct khanates, each carving out its own legacy upon the steppes and beyond. Here, in the heart of the four Khanates — the Yuan, the Golden Horde, the Chagatai, and the Ilkhanate — the intricate dance of power and culture played out, revealing the complexity of Mongol rule post-Genghis.

But why delve into the absorptive chapters of these divided realms? The answer lies in the fabric of their interwoven fates, the mingling of blood and ambition, and the sway they held over the world. By examining the silken threads of similarity that bound them, yet also the sharp contrasts that defined their identities, one may glean insights into the grander narrative of empire and human endeavor.

The benchmarks for our scrutiny lie in governance, culture, economic policy, and foreign relations. These facets act as mirrors, reflecting the essence of each khanate's character and their place in the greater mosaic of history.

When one conjures the image of the Yuan Dynasty, it is the grandeur of Kublai's court that flickers to life, a realm where the Mongol spirit was tempered by the influences of the settled civilizations it encompassed. In contrast, stand the Golden Horde, their dominion stretching over the vast Russian steppes, where Mongol tradition rode on, unbridled by the sedentary cultures. The Chagatai Khanate, nestled in Central Asia, remained truer to the nomadic lifestyle, while the Ilkhanate, reaching across Persia and the Middle East, became a melting pot of Mongol military might and cultural sophistication.

Each khanate, like the branches of a mighty tree, shared the same Mongol roots. They wielded the composite bow with equal deadly grace, and their horses thundered with the same fervor, carrying forth the legacy of their ancestors' unparalleled cavalry. Their administrative systems, too, bore the hallmark of Mongol pragmatism, with the yassa — Genghis Khan's code of laws — serving as the backbone of governance across the disparate realms.

Still, the divergence was stark, as vivid as the hues at the close of day. The Yuan Dynasty, embracing the Chinese bureaucratic system, flourished as a beacon of administration and culture, whereas the

Golden Horde, ruling over a mosaic of subjugated peoples, relied on a system of tribute that kept them at an arm's length from direct governance. The Chagatai lands grappled with internal strife and fluctuating leadership, and the Ilkhanate thrived as a crucible of cultural and religious exchange, its rulers even flirting with the notion of Christianity for political alliance.

Imagine, if you will, the bustling markets of Tabriz under Ilkhanate rule, where Persian merchants haggled beneath the watchful eyes of Mongol guards. Could the air have been thick with the aroma of exotic spices and the din of diverse tongues, a testament to the Ilkhanate's role in the Silk Road's symphony of trade?

The analysis of these entities reveals the adaptability of the Mongol identity, its ability to assimilate and be assimilated. Yet, it also underscores the centrifugal forces of ambition and geography that tugged at the seams of empire, pulling the khanates into their unique orbits.

In the contemporary lens, the legacy of the Mongol Khanates finds resonance in the very notion of a fragmented world coming together through the forces of globalization. Their narratives offer a prelude to modern issues of governance, cultural integration, and economic interdependence.

One-line paragraphs, like solitary sentinels, stand to punctuate the gravity of our inquiry: What do the fates of the Khanates teach us about the unity and division of empires?

In the fading echoes of Mongol hoofbeats and the whispers of silk-laden breezes, the Khanates speak to us of an age where the splintering of a colossus birthed new worlds. Their story is a saga of shared blood and divergent paths, of empires that rose from the division of a mightier whole, and in doing so, shaped the course of history.

Thus, the division of the Mongol Empire into the Khanates is not merely a tale of separation but a narrative rich with the interplay of continuity and change. As the pages of history turn, the echoes of the past ask us to consider how the divisions of today might shape the legacies of tomorrow.

The Imperial Capital: Karakorum

IN THE HEART OF THE Mongol Empire, a city emerged from the steppes like a vision etched in the minds of the nomads who once traversed the vast Eurasian plains. This city was Karakorum, the imperial capital, a linchpin of power and a crucible of culture that stood as a testament to the empire's grandeur. Its very name, Karakorum, resonates with the legacy of a people who, under the banner of Genghis Khan, forged the largest contiguous land empire in history.

Karakorum, in its essence, was the physical manifestation of the Mongol Empire's might and the epicenter of its political and cultural life. It was established by Genghis Khan in the early 13th century and later developed by his successors, particularly by Ögedei Khan, who envisioned it as the empire's administrative heart. To define Karakorum succinctly, it was the imperial capital from which the Mongols administered their vast territories and orchestrated their military campaigns.

The city's key elements included the grand palace of the khans, the impressive silver tree crafted by the Parisian goldsmith Guillaume Bouchier, and the various religious institutions that dotted its landscape. Karakorum was a melting pot of religious diversity, housing Christians, Muslims, Buddhists, and followers of the ancient Tengri faith. This religious plurality symbolized the Mongols' pragmatic approach to governance.

Delving into the historical context, Karakorum's significance was not solely due to its architectural achievements or political importance. Rather, it was a beacon of the Pax Mongolica, the period of relative peace that the Mongol governance brought to the regions under its sway. This peace facilitated trade, communication, and cultural exchanges across Eurasia, with Karakorum at its nexus.

When contextualized within the broader framework of the empire, Karakorum can be seen as the nerve center from which the Mongols projected their power. It was from here that the yam, an intricate system of relay stations that enabled swift communication across the empire, was managed. The city also played host to foreign dignitaries and merchants, becoming a vibrant hub where ideas and goods flowed as freely as the waters of the nearby Orkhon River.

Examples of Karakorum's significance in real-world applications abound. One could cite the diplomatic missions it welcomed, such as those led by the Franciscan friar William of Rubruck or the chronicler Marco Polo, whose accounts provide rich descriptions of life in the capital. Their narratives paint a picture of a bustling, cosmopolitan city where East met West in a dynamic exchange of cultures and commodities.

Common misconceptions about Karakorum may depict it as a permanent, stone-laden metropolis typical of contemporary capitals. However, this view overlooks the Mongol's nomadic heritage, which influenced the city's development. While parts of Karakorum were indeed constructed of stone and brick, much of it retained a transient quality, with gers (yurts) forming a significant aspect of its urban landscape, reflecting the Mongols' enduring connection to their nomadic roots.

Now, let us ponder for a moment: What might life have been like for a common trader entering Karakorum's gates? Would he have marveled at the sight of the silver tree, its roots drawing water from a nearby stream, or found himself lost in the maze of market stalls, each brimming with the riches of the Silk Road?

In the prose of this narrative, a one-line paragraph emerges to assert its significance: Karakorum was the heart of an empire that changed the world.

The use of vivid imagery transports us to the imperial city's streets, where the clangor of blacksmiths mingling with the chants of Buddhist monks creates a symphony of civilization. Through careful choice of words, simplicity in language, and attention to cadence, the essence of Karakorum is distilled into a form that the reader can almost perceive with their senses.

Dialogue from the era, though scarce, can be imagined through the accounts of visitors, such as when William of Rubruck expressed his astonishment at the city's diversity, saying, "I have seen there people from every nation who have been brought there by the affairs of the Tartar court."

Ultimately, the portrayal of Karakorum should not merely recount its splendors and significance; it should also evoke a vivid tableau of an empire at its zenith. To show, not just tell, the reader must be immersed in the lifeblood of the city, its thrumming vitality, and its role as the beating heart of an empire whose legacy continues to reverberate through history.

Mongol Influence on the World

The Silk Road Under Mongol Rule

Throughout history, few conduits of trade and culture have been as significant as the Silk Road. This ancient network of trade routes connected the vibrant worlds of East and West, an artery of commerce and exchange that pulsed with life for centuries. But what were the elements that contributed to its flourishing, especially under the dominion of the Mongol Empire? Let us unfurl the scrolls of history and trace the evolution of this legendary route under the watchful eyes of the Mongols.

In the beginning, the Silk Road was less a road and more a series of trodden paths, carved by the hooves of nomadic traders. As early as the 2nd century BCE, these trails began to weave together, linking the imperial power of China with the distant lands of Rome. The desire for the luxurious silk of the East set the stage for an exchange that would grow to include not only goods but also ideas, religions, and technologies.

The chronicles of the Silk Road are etched with milestones, each a testament to its enduring legacy. The conquests of Alexander the Great in the 4th century BCE extended Greek influence to Central Asia, setting the precursor for later exchanges. Then came the Han Dynasty's push to establish trade, culminating in the missions of Zhang Qian, who opened the gates to the Western regions.

But it was under the indomitable shadow of the Mongol Empire, from the 13th to the 14th century, that the Silk Road truly reached its zenith. The Mongols, led first by the legendary Genghis Khan, forged an empire that spanned from the Pacific to the Adriatic Sea. With this unprecedented unification came peace—the Pax Mongolica—allowing trade to thrive.

Imagine, if you will, vast caravans wending through mountain passes, laden with spices, textiles, and precious stones. Can you see the colorful bazaars, hear the cacophony of languages, and smell the mingling scents of exotic wares? These were the days when the Silk Road burgeoned under the protection of the Mongol khans. Their enforcement of security, standardization of trade laws, and patronage of merchants facilitated an era of prosperity and cultural exchange.

The route's trajectory differed from region to region, adapting to the contours of empires, deserts, and mountains. In the heart of Central Asia, it branched out, weaving a web of paths through cities like Samarkand and Bukhara, each a jewel with its own unique cultural blend. In the Middle East, the Silk Road absorbed the various flavors of culture, while in Europe, it touched the fringes of emerging powers like Venice, whose merchants, such as Marco Polo, would become legendary for their travels to the East.

Modern interpretations of the Silk Road often romanticize its golden age under the Mongols, yet the route has never truly fallen into dormancy. The legacy of the Silk Road endures in the cultural and genetic imprints left on the regions it touched. Today, the concept has been reborn in the form of China's Belt and Road Initiative, a bold plan to recreate the trade networks of old, albeit in a modern geopolitical landscape fraught with new challenges and controversies.

But what of the turning points, the moments when the Silk Road teetered on the brink of oblivion? The decline of the Mongol Empire sowed the seeds of fragmentation, and as maritime trade routes gained prominence, the overland caravans waned. Yet, did the Silk Road ever truly die, or did it simply evolve to match the rhythm of a changing world?

In considering the grand scope of the Silk Road's history, one might ask: what lessons does its past hold for our present, and how might its spirit of cultural exchange inform our future? As we ponder these questions, let us not forget the enduring legacy of the Mongol Empire in shaping a world where, for a brief, shining moment, the distant corners of the earth were connected by the silken threads of commerce and mutual curiosity.

Pax Mongolica: An Era of Stability

DIVING INTO THE HEART of the Pax Mongolica, it becomes apparent that to truly grasp the nuance of this period, one must become acquainted with the vernacular of the era. These terms are the keys to unlocking a deeper understanding of the Mongol Empire's influence on Eurasian trade and culture.

A compendium of such terms would include Pax Mongolica, Yassa, Yam system, Karakorum, and the Silk Road itself. Each of these words carries weight, their meanings intertwined with the history that the Mongol Empire wove across continents.

The term "Pax Mongolica," reminiscent of the Roman Pax Romana, refers to the span of relative peace that the Mongol Empire instilled across much of Eurasia during the 13th and 14th centuries. But how did a nomadic people, once perceived as the scourge of civilizations, foster an environment where peace could flourish? This paradox beckons a closer examination.

Integral to this stability was "Yassa," the code of laws imposed by Genghis Khan and his successors. More than just a set of rules, Yassa was the glue that held the empire's diverse peoples together, merging customary steppe laws with the various customs of subjugated lands. It was a legal framework that, among other things, prioritized the safety of foreign merchants and envoys, thereby lubricating the wheels of trade.

The "Yam system" was another cornerstone of Mongol governance—a relay network of stations and couriers that facilitated communication across the empire's vast expanse. Picture a series of nodes, each within a day's ride of the next, ensuring that messages and goods could travel with unprecedented speed. This system was not unlike the internet of the medieval world, a comparison that might kindle a flame of recognition in the modern mind.

Karakorum, the empire's capital, stood as a symbol of Mongol power and cosmopolitanism. Under the blue skies of the Mongolian steppe, this city drew intellectuals, artisans, and religious figures from every corner of the known world. Karakorum was more than a political center; it was a crucible of cultures, an ancient melting pot where ideas and traditions blended under the watchful eyes of stone turtles guarding its gates.

Lastly, the Silk Road—a term coined long after the Mongols' time—refers to the network of trade routes that connected Asia with Europe. Under the Pax Mongolica, this road thrived like never before. Its very name evokes the luxurious fabric that became the emblem of exchange between East and West, but in truth, it carried far more than silk, serving as the conduit for an astonishing variety of goods and wisdom.

Can you imagine the bustling markets along these routes? The air would be rich with the scent of cinnamon, cloves, and cardamom, mingling with the rugged smell of the camels and the musky odor of the felt yurts. These markets were not just centers of commerce but hubs of human interaction where languages, beliefs, and technologies were exchanged as freely as the goods for sale.

This period of stability, however, was more than an era of economic prosperity. It was a time when the arts flourished, when astronomy, medicine, and engineering were subjects of passionate discourse in the courts of Mongol rulers. These khans, once seen as destroyers, became patrons of culture, inadvertently seeding the Renaissance that would later bloom in Europe.

In this context, the Pax Mongolica was not merely a pause in the chaos of history. It was a canvas on which humanity painted a masterpiece of interaction and exchange. The Mongols did not create culture; rather, they created the conditions under which culture could thrive, connecting disparate worlds with silken threads and iron decrees.

The might of the Mongol Empire eventually waned, its dominion fractured by succession disputes and the relentless march of time. Yet the legacy of the Pax Mongolica endures. It stands as a testament to the power of unity and the potential of diverse cultures to coalesce into something greater than the sum of their parts.

As we traverse the annals of history, contemplating the rise and fall of empires, we might find ourselves pondering the nature of peace and stability. What does it take to forge a period of tranquility amidst the tumult of human ambition? How can the lessons of the past inform the ceaseless quest for harmony in our own tumultuous times?

The Mongol Empire, with all its contradictions, offers a narrative rife with complexity and a multitude of stories waiting to be told. This empire, which once ruled the largest contiguous landmass in history, bequeathed to the world a time of unparalleled connectivity. It reminds us that even the most unlikely of empires can engender a legacy that resonates through the ages, echoing in the pages of history and the corridors of our collective memory.

Mongol Warfare and European Knights

WHEN IT COMES TO MILITARY history, few contrasts are as stark or as instructive as that between the cavalry of the Mongol hordes and the armored knights of Medieval Europe. These warriors, emblematic of their respective cultures, engaged in combat strategies that, while often divergent, reveal a shared mastery of the battlefield suited to their time and place.

Why, one may inquire, should the approach of the Mongols to warfare be juxtaposed with the martial traditions of European chivalry? The pursuit of this comparison is not mere academic fancy; it provides a lens through which to view the broader implications of military innovation and adaptation.

To dissect these military giants, one must establish criteria that encompass the breadth of their martial prowess. Considerations must be given to their tactical approaches, organizational structures, equipment, and the societal values that informed their conduct in war.

At first glance, similarities abound. Both Mongol warriors and European knights were cavalrymen, reliant upon the horse. Their reputations were built upon mobility and the shock value of a well-timed charge. On horseback, they inspired fear and commanded respect, each a testament to the power of a mounted force in the open field.

Yet, delve deeper, and the distinctions begin to overshadow these surface-level similitudes. The Mongol cavalry was a force of exceptional mobility and endurance, capable of covering vast distances at speed that European counterparts could scarcely fathom. Their horses, hardy steppe ponies, were less imposing than the destriers of Europe, but they were well-suited to the rigors of campaign life on the steppes of Asia.

In stark contrast, the European knight was a product of feudal society, his armor heavy, his charge thunderous. Encased in chainmail or plate, the knight was a moving fortress, his presence on the battlefield as much a psychological weapon as a physical one.

Visualize, if you will, the Mongol archer, mounted, drawing his composite bow with an ease born of lifelong practice. His arrows could rain down upon foes with precision and at a range that made the most of his steed's agility. European knights, in their turn, were more often than not, practitioners of the lance and sword, their combat style up close and personal, their charge designed to break the enemy line with brute force.

What insights do these comparisons yield? The Mongol reliance on horse archery allowed them to execute complex maneuvers, such as the feigned retreat, which bewildered and decimated their adversaries. The knights, bound by chivalric codes, often sought glory in direct confrontation, a method that, while honorable, had its limitations against more unorthodox strategies.

The organizational genius of the Mongols also stands in sharp relief against the feudal levies of Europe. The Mongol military was a meritocracy, its leaders chosen for skill rather than birthright. Their units, the tumens, were highly disciplined formations of 10,000, capable of operating independently or as part of a larger force. European armies, meanwhile, were often composed of vassals and their retainers, their allegiance to their lord as important as their allegiance to their king or cause.

Does this not prompt one to ponder the broader implications of such differences? The Mongols, under the unifying vision of Genghis Khan, created an empire that spanned continents, their military acumen enabling them to conquer disparate peoples and terrains. The knights of Europe, for all their valor, were often embroiled in localized conflicts, their military practices as much a reflection of their societal structure as of their battlefield requirements.

In the modern world, the legacy of these martial traditions continues to resonate. The emphasis on mobility, precision, and adaptability championed by the Mongols finds its echoes in contemporary doctrines of maneuver warfare. The knightly focus on heavy armor and direct assault lives on in the use of armored vehicles and the doctrine of shock action.

As the pages of history turn, the tales of Mongol cavalries and European knights remain etched into our collective consciousness, their strategies and exploits continuing to inform military thought and practice. The comparison of these two formidable forces is not merely an exercise in historical curiosity but a dialogue with the past, one that holds perennial lessons for the art of war.

The Mongol Empire and the knights of Europe, each in their own right, were architects of their age, their approaches to warfare a dance of innovation and tradition.

The Mongol Influence on Russia

THE VAST EXPANSE OF the Russian steppes lay open, a land of harsh winters and fertile summers, home to a myriad of Slavic tribes and nascent principalities. This was the stage upon which the Mongol Empire would cast its long shadow, forging a tumultuous relationship that would shape the destiny of Russia for centuries.

Genghis Khan's successors, the khans of the Golden Horde, were the principal figures who orchestrated this sweeping historical drama. Their influence, though wielded with a heavy hand, would leave an indelible mark on the fabric of Russian statehood and culture. Among these Mongol leaders, Batu Khan, a grandson of Genghis Khan, was the architect of the Mongol dominance over the Rus' territories, setting in motion a saga of subjugation and integration that is as complex as it is profound.

The core challenge faced by the Russian principalities was no less than survival in the face of the Mongol onslaught. The Mongol Empire, at the zenith of its power, was an unstoppable force, wielding strategies of warfare so advanced and ruthless that they seemed an elemental force of nature. The Russian princes, fragmented and often at odds with one another, found themselves ill-prepared for the storm that was to descend upon them.

To meet this existential threat, the Russian principalities were compelled to adapt. Their approach to this dire situation was multifaceted, a blend of resistance, subterfuge, accommodation, and, over time, assimilation of certain Mongol practices. The strategies employed by the Russians ranged from military engagements, such as the Battle of the Kalka River, to the more pragmatic payment of tribute, which, while galling, ensured a measure of autonomy under the "Tatar Yoke."

The results of these adaptive strategies were as varied as they were profound. On the one hand, the Mongol occupation stifled the growth of Russian territories and subjected the populace to heavy tributes and the whims of foreign khans. However, it also inadvertently led to the centralization of power in the hands of the Grand Princes of Moscow, who positioned themselves as the chief intermediaries between the Mongol overlords and the other Russian rulers. Moscow's ascendancy would, in time, lay the groundwork for the rise of the Russian Empire.

Reflecting on this historical episode, one must grapple with the paradoxical nature of the Mongol influence. The Mongol governance model, with its emphasis on meritocracy and religious tolerance, left its imprint on Russian administrative practices. Yet, the brutality of Mongol rule and the imposition of their dominion cannot be understated. The cultural exchange was significant, with the Russian language absorbing Mongol words and the art of war evolving in response to the Mongol tactics.

Visual aids depicting the Mongol military encampments, the trade routes established during their reign, and the evolving Russian principalities would serve to illustrate the deep interconnection between the occupiers and the subjugated, enriching the reader's understanding of this complex historical tapestry.

The Mongol occupation of Russia was not an isolated event but a transformative period that connected to the larger narrative of Mongol expansion and Eurasian history. The Mongol Empire served as a conduit for the exchange of ideas, goods, and technologies between East and West, with Russia acting as a crucial frontier in this vast network.

As we close this chapter, one might ponder how the legacy of the Mongol Empire continues to reverberate through the corridors of Russian history. Did the Mongol rule hinder or hasten the emergence of the Russian state? In what ways did the crucible of the Mongol occupation forge the indomitable spirit of the Russian people, a spirit that has weathered invasions and upheavals through the ages?

The Mongol influence on Russia is a saga of conquest and resilience, of cultural amalgamation and the relentless pursuit of sovereignty. It is a narrative rich in lessons, echoing through time, reminding us that the forces that shape nations are as complex as they are enduring. As history buffs, we delve into these depths, seeking not just to recount tales of yore but to understand the currents that shape the present and the future. What insights might we gain from this chapter of history that can illuminate the paths we tread today?

The Transmission of Knowledge

THE MONGOL EMPIRE, a colossal force that once commanded the largest contiguous land empire in history, was not just a machine of conquest and subjugation. Beyond the might of horse and bow, lay a lesser-known but equally powerful tool: the transmission of knowledge. As the Mongols swept across Asia and into Europe, they became inadvertent harbingers of an intellectual renaissance, the scope and impact of which still resonates today.

The empire, under the rule of Genghis Khan and his successors, was extraordinary not only for its military prowess but also for its promotion of trade, communication, and the exchange of ideas across vast distances. The Mongols, often viewed through a lens of barbarism, were, in fact, instrumental in the dissemination of scientific, technological, and cultural knowledge throughout their territories. They fostered an environment where scholars, artisans, and traders from diverse backgrounds could mingle and share their insights, thereby enhancing the collective understanding of the world.

At the heart of this claim lies the Mongol's establishment of the Silk Road. These routes served as the lifeblood of exchange, where not only goods but also knowledge traveled. But was this merely a byproduct of commerce, or did the Mongols intentionally cultivate the spread of knowledge?

Primary evidence of the Mongols' deliberate efforts to facilitate intellectual exchange comes from their policy of religious tolerance and their patronage of the arts and sciences. The Mongol khans, such as Kublai Khan, welcomed astronomers, mathematicians, and engineers from various societies, European lands, and the Far East into their courts. They sought experts in various fields to help administer their empire and enhance its splendor. The Ilkhanate, for instance, saw the translation of astronomical works from Persian and Arabic into Mongolian and the establishment of observatories in cities like Maragheh. These acts were not mere coincidences but calculated steps towards accumulating and centralizing knowledge.

To delve deeper, the Mongol postal system, the Yam, revolutionized communication across Eurasia. It facilitated the swift and reliable transfer of information, allowing for the exchange of ideas across cultures and disciplines. Through the Yam, Chinese advances in printing and papermaking spread to the West.

However, the picture was not entirely rosy. Some historians present counter-evidence, suggesting that the Mongols, in their quest for domination, destroyed much of the infrastructure that supported learning, including libraries, universities, and entire cities. The sacking of Baghdad in 1258 is often cited as a calamity, leading to the loss of countless manuscripts and scholarly works.

In response to such counterarguments, it's crucial to clarify that while the Mongols did indeed wreak havoc in many regions, their overall impact on knowledge transmission was not uniformly destructive. Following initial conquests, the Mongols often built upon the ruins, creating new centers of learning and facilitating the restoration of cultural and intellectual life. The Pax Mongolica, a period of relative peace and stability under Mongol rule, allowed for safer travel and trade, promoting a remarkable cultural and intellectual flourishing.

Furthermore, the introduction of paper currency under the Mongols revolutionized trade, enabling the movement of wealth without the physical burden of precious metals. This innovation had far-reaching economic and cultural implications, supporting the activities of merchants and scholars alike.

The conclusion, reinforced by the weight of historical evidence, is that the Mongol Empire was a catalyst for the spread of knowledge across the known world. The Mongols' policies and innovations laid the groundwork for an interconnected world, where ideas could traverse borders and oceans, seeding the early beginnings of a globalized society.

One must pause to wonder, what if the Mongol Empire had not risen to power and connected East with West in such a profound way? Would the Renaissance have bloomed with the same vibrancy without the influx of knowledge from the East? These questions invite us to reflect on the intricate web of causality that history weaves.

In sum, the Mongol Empire's role in the transmission of knowledge is an epic journey across the tapestry of human endeavor. It is a story of how a nomadic warrior tribe not only conquered lands but also bridged worlds, fostering an era of intellectual and cultural exchange that enlightened the dark corners of medieval ignorance. This narrative, etched in the annals of history, stands as a testament to the power of connectivity and the enduring legacy of the Mongol Empire as a force for knowledge and progress.

The Empire's Zenith and the Turn of Tide

The Last Great Khan: Timur

In the year 1402, the dusty plains of Anatolia bore witness to a clash of titans. As the sun scorched the earth, the air hummed with the tension of impending battle. It was here, at the Battle of Ankara, where the fates of empires would intertwine, and the aspirations of a man who saw himself as the heir to Genghis Khan would be tested against the might of the Ottoman Sultan.

The figure at the heart of this story, Timur—also known as Tamerlane—stood resolute on a raised knoll, surveying the vast expanse before him. His confident gaze betrayed no hint of the injury that had crippled his leg, earning him the moniker 'Timur the Lame'. But it was not his physical form that struck fear into the hearts of his enemies; it was the sharpness of his mind, the unyielding will that commanded legions, and the dream that drove him—a dream to resurrect the glory of the Mongol Empire.

Timur's journey to this critical juncture was as unpredictable as the path of a stray arrow in battle. Born into the Barlas tribe, a Mongolic group that had settled in Transoxiana (modern-day Uzbekistan), he rose from obscurity through a combination of astute political maneuvering and military prowess. But what truly set him apart was his unquenchable thirst for more: more land, more power, and an insatiable desire to etch his name alongside the great Khans of the past.

As the two armies collided in a maelstrom of steel and horseflesh, Timur's strategic genius shone through. His forces, though outnumbered, were a hardened reflection of his own resilience. They were the anvil upon which the fate of the Ottoman Sultan Bayezid I would be forged. In the end, the Sultan was captured, his forces scattered like leaves in the wind. The world took notice: Timur was not just a warlord, he was a force of history.

But what does one find in the heart of such a man? Glimpses of his inner world revealed an enigma—a leader who adorned his capital, Samarkand, with the spoils of conquest, yet whose own desires remained as austere as the steppes of his youth. He was both a patron of the arts and a ruthless conqueror. His rule was marked by the dualities of enlightenment and savagery, vision and brutality.

The unexpected turn in Timur's tale came not from his enemies, but from his own mortality. In the midst of preparing to invade China, death claimed him in 1405. The empire he had built, stretching from the sands of Syria to the gates of Delhi, began to crumble without him. Yet, his legacy endured, as a reminder of what one man's ambition could achieve and the impermanence of even the grandest of empires.

The Black Death: A Blow to Empire

IN THE MID-14TH CENTURY, a shadow more menacing than the mightiest of armies began to spread across the vast expanse of the Eurasian continent. It was an invisible harbinger of doom that would come to be known as the Black Death. This relentless plague, carried on the backs of fleas that infested the black rats aboard the trade caravans, found an unwitting ally in the interconnected routes fostered by the Pax Mongolica. The Mongol Empire, at the zenith of its power, facilitating trade between the distant corners of the world, was about to face a foe that knew no borders, respected no authority, and wielded a deadly force that could cripple empires.

The problem was insidious; the bubonic plague did not discriminate between rich and poor, soldier or civilian. The Mongol Empire, with its vast populations and highly mobile society, was particularly vulnerable. The plague decimated its population, leaving ghost towns in its wake. The once bustling cities became silent mausoleums of a bygone era. The very fabric of the empire, woven together by the threads of trade and military conquest, began to unravel as the disease took its toll on the populace and the economy.

The consequences of ignoring this calamity were dire. The depopulation meant fewer soldiers to defend the empire's far-flung borders and maintain order. It meant less manpower to cultivate the fields and to engage in the trade that had enriched the empire. The trade routes became conduits of death rather than wealth, and fear stifled the movement of goods and people. The military, the cornerstone of Mongol power, was not immune; the ranks thinned as the plague claimed the lives of countless warriors.

In the face of such an adversary, the solution demanded a multifaceted approach. The empire needed to quarantine affected areas to contain the spread of the disease. This would be a departure from the ethos of openness that characterized the Pax Mongolica, but it was necessary for survival. Measures to promote hygiene and sanitation in the military and among the populace could slow the plague's momentum. Furthermore, diversifying economic activities beyond trade could mitigate the impact of disrupted commerce.

Implementing these solutions required swift and decisive action. Quarantine zones would need to be established with strict controls on movement. Public health initiatives, such as burning the belongings of the deceased and enforcing the regular cleaning of streets and disposal of waste, must be enforced. Economic resilience could be fostered by encouraging local production and stockpiling essential goods.

Evidence of the efficacy of such measures can be drawn from later pandemics where isolation and hygiene practices played crucial roles in managing outbreaks. The success of these interventions in more recent history offers a glimpse of how the Mongol Empire might have mitigated the devastation wrought by the Black Death.

While the primary solution focused on containment and public health, alternative strategies were also conceivable. The empire might have expanded its medical knowledge by seeking remedies and treatments from the far reaches of its territories, incorporating the wisdom of different cultures under its rule. This, too, was a double-edged sword, as travel to seek such knowledge could further spread the disease, but if managed carefully, it could have offered hope and potential cures.

The Mongol Empire's encounter with the Black Death was a clash of two titanic forces, one built on the power of conquest and the other an unyielding natural disaster. The outcome was a lesson in the vulnerability of even the mightiest of empires to the capricious whims of nature.

But ponder this, reader: what might have transpired had the Mongols possessed the foresight to address the plague proactively? Could the empire that stretched from the Pacific to the heart of Europe have withstood the ravages of the Black Death and maintained its dominance over the known world? These questions invite us to consider the delicate balance of power and the unforeseen events that can alter the course of history.

The story of the Mongol Empire and the Black Death is a testament to the fragility of human achievements. It is a tale of resilience in the face of unimaginable adversity, a narrative that unfolds with the inexorable march of time and the echoes of once-great cities now silenced. It reminds us that in the grand theater of history, no empire is immune to the forces that conspire to shape its destiny.

Internal Conflicts and Fragmentation

AMIDST THE SILENT CITIES and the lingering shadow of the Black Death, the Mongol Empire faced yet another formidable challenge from within. The sprawling empire, once tightly held together under the unyielding grip of Genghis Khan, began to show signs of internal strain as power struggles and succession disputes gnawed at its foundations.

The inception of these internal conflicts can be traced back to the very nature of Mongol succession. Genghis Khan's death in 1227 left a void that was temporarily filled by his capable successors. However, the seeds of discord were sown with the tradition of the kurultai, the grand assembly that selected the Great Khan. It was a system based on merit and consensus among the Mongol elites, but it also laid the groundwork for future fracturing as the empire expanded and the distances between its rulers grew.

The first significant milestone in the empire's fragmentation came with the death of Möngke Khan in 1259. His demise set off a succession crisis that pitted brother against brother in a struggle for supremacy. The once unified Mongol forces found themselves embroiled in a civil war, with Hulagu Khan and Kublai Khan emerging as the main contenders for the title of Great Khan. The conflict would lead to the formal splitting of the empire into distinct khanates: Ilkhanate, Golden Horde, Chagatai Khanate, and the Yuan dynasty in China, each ruled by a descendant of Genghis Khan.

As the empire fractured, cultural and regional variations began to surface. Each khanate adopted the customs and religions of the lands they ruled, drifting further from the traditional Mongol way of life. The Ilkhanate in Persia, for example, saw its rulers convert to Islam, which led to further divisions with the staunchly shamanistic or Buddhist segments of the empire.

The modern interpretations of these events shed light on the complexity of Mongol governance. Historians debate the extent to which these internal conflicts were inevitable, given the empire's rapid expansion and the logistical difficulties in maintaining control over such vast territories. The Mongols had conquered a multitude of diverse cultures, and the challenge of integrating these into a single political entity was daunting. It is a testament to their initial success that the empire lasted as long as it did before succumbing to these inherent tensions.

Challenges and controversies continue to surround discussions of the Mongol Empire's decline. Some argue that the very nature of the Mongol military, with its emphasis on mobility and speed, was ill-suited to the static administration of vast domains. Others point to the failure of the Mongols to establish a sustainable economic framework that could support the empire in times of peace as much as in war.

One cannot help but ponder the what-ifs. What if the Mongols had developed a more robust system for succession, one that could withstand the ambitions of rival princes? What if they had found a way to bridge the cultural divides that emerged within their empire?

In the end, the Mongol Empire's decline was as meteoric as its rise. The fragmentation that began with succession disputes culminated in a period where the once mighty Mongol hordes were reduced to warring factions, each seeking to preserve their own power. The empire that had changed the face of the world was now a collection of smaller states, each bearing the legacy of Mongol rule in their military tactics, trade practices, and cultural exchanges.

The story of the Mongol Empire is a rich tale of conquest, innovation, and ultimately, disintegration. It serves as a powerful reminder of the transience of power and the ever-present dangers of internal discord. As the empire faded, the world entered a new era, one shaped by the cultural diffusion and the vast trade networks the Mongols had once established. The echoes of their rule can still be heard in the languages, religions, and customs of the many peoples they once dominated, a legacy that endures beyond the empire's demise.

The Fall of the Yuan Dynasty

IN THE HEART OF THE Middle Kingdom, the Yuan dynasty, established by the illustrious Kublai Khan, reigned with might and majesty over the vast expanses of China. It was an era marked by monumental achievements, from the construction of the grand capital at Dadu (modern-day Beijing) to the flourishing of trade along the Silk Road. Yet, beneath the surface of these grandiose accomplishments, the seeds of discord were sprouting, foretelling the empire's eventual collapse.

At the center of this unfolding drama were the Mongol rulers, foreign conquerors who had seized the Chinese throne. Though their reign brought about an unprecedented fusion of cultures, it also sowed the roots of their downfall. The Mongols maintained a distinct identity, preferring to rule over the Han Chinese majority from a distance, which only served to widen the chasm between ruler and subject.

The challenge that would ultimately bring the Yuan dynasty to its knees was multifaceted. It stemmed from a toxic brew of administrative corruption, internal rebellion, external pressures, and a series of natural disasters that battered the empire's already weakened foundations. These calamities, coupled with the devastating impact of the Black Death, left the Yuan dynasty vulnerable and reeling.

The Mongols, famed for their military prowess, had built their empire on the back of their horse-mounted warriors. Yet, they faced an insurmountable challenge when it came to governance. The empire's vastness required a level of administrative sophistication that the Mongols struggled to maintain. Their approach to solving this dilemma was to import foreign administrators, which only served to further alienate the Chinese populace.

As the empire buckled under the weight of its own complexity, a new force emerged from the shadows. The Red Turban Rebellion, a movement driven by the White Lotus Society, tapped into the widespread discontent. The Mongols, in response, employed a series of brutal crackdowns, but these measures only fanned the flames of resistance.

The results of the Mongol efforts were a dismal failure. The Red Turban Rebellion gained momentum, leading to the ascendancy of the Ming dynasty. The Mongol rulers, once the terror of the known world, were forced to retreat to their heartland in the steppe, their dreams of ruling China shattered.

In retrospect, the fall of the Yuan dynasty offers profound insights into the delicate balance required to maintain an empire. The Mongols, who had so adeptly conquered vast lands, could not mold themselves into the stationary bureaucrats required to sustain their conquests. Their failure was not merely military; it was a failure to adapt, to weave together the disparate threads of their empire into a cohesive whole.

The Yuan dynasty's downfall is a single thread in the larger narrative of the Mongol Empire's fragmentation. It serves as a cautionary tale of the impermanence of power and the inevitable decline that follows when rulers become disconnected from the governed.

As the last of the Yuan emperors fled the imperial palace, one cannot help but ponder the ironies of history. How did the mighty Mongols, who had once forged the largest contiguous empire in human history, find themselves cast down from the pinnacle of power?

The Fall of the Yuan Dynasty is not just a tale of an empire's demise; it is a reflection on the nature of power, governance, and the human spirit. It is a story that compels us to question the very essence of leadership and the responsibilities that come with immense authority. How might the course of history have changed if the Mongols had embraced the complexities of ruling a settled empire as deftly as they had mastered the art of war?

In the final analysis, the legacy of the Mongols in China is etched into the very fabric of its history—a legacy of grandeur and ruin, of conquest and loss. The Yuan dynasty's fall from grace is a poignant reminder that even the mightiest empires are not immune to the tides of change. And as we turn the page, we are left to contemplate the enduring impact of their rule on the civilization that followed in their wake.

Culture and Society in the Mongol Empire

Nomadic Lifestyle: The Heart of the Empire

In the vast steppe lands of Central Asia, under the endless blue sky, the Mongol Empire arose, not merely as a political entity but as a manifestation of a way of life that had weathered the harshness of the region for centuries. The heart of this empire was not forged from stone or iron but from the nomadic traditions that shaped its people and their approach to life, war, and governance.

At the core of Mongol society was a term that might seem deceptively simple yet encapsulated a complex system: the nomadic lifestyle. This was not merely a matter of moving from place to place but a sophisticated mode of existence, finely tuned to the rhythms of nature and the needs of the community.

A nomadic lifestyle can be defined as a way of life in which a group moves from one place to another, rather than settling permanently in one location. For the Mongols, this meant a continuous cycle of migration in search of grazing land for their horses and livestock, which were central to their survival and culture. It was a life that necessitated portable housing, such as the ger (also known as a yurt), and a deep understanding of the environment.

Key elements of this nomadic existence included horsemanship, archery, and animal husbandry. The Mongols were unparalleled horsemen, each warrior capable of riding for days without rest and skilled in the art of mounted combat. Their bows, crafted from a composite of materials, could shoot with accuracy and power, making them formidable on the battlefield. The rearing of livestock such as sheep, goats, and camels provided not only sustenance but materials for clothing, shelter, and tools.

While the exact origins of this nomadic culture are shrouded in the mists of time, it is believed that the harsh conditions of the steppe itself necessitated a mobile way of life. The word "nomad" comes from the Greek "nomas," meaning "roaming in search of pasture." This etymology hints at the deep relationship between the Mongols and their environment.

Placing the nomadic lifestyle of the Mongols within a broader framework, it becomes evident how this way of life was instrumental in the formation and expansion of their empire. The mobility of their society allowed for rapid military deployment, the ability to traverse great distances with ease, and a system of communication that was unparalleled in its time. The Mongols could strike swiftly, like a storm over the steppes, and then vanish just as quickly, confounding their more sedentary adversaries.

The real-world applications of the nomadic lifestyle extended to trade and diplomacy as well. As mentioned earlier in this book, the Mongols established extensive trade routes, connecting East with West, and their caravans carried not only goods but ideas, technologies, and cultural practices.

One might wonder how such a seemingly transient way of life could lead to the establishment of the largest contiguous land empire in history. The answer lies in the adaptability and resilience of the Mongol people. Their ability to live off the land, to endure and even thrive in extreme conditions, was the bedrock upon which they built their military and political might.

However, common misconceptions about the nomadic lifestyle abound. It's often misinterpreted as primitive or disorganized, when, in reality, it required a sophisticated understanding of logistics, resource management, and social cohesion.

Have you ever considered the intricate balance between freedom and survival that the nomadic lifestyle entails?

The simplicity of the Mongol way of life belies its complexity. The ger, for instance, is not just a tent but a portable home that could be dismantled and reassembled quickly, an embodiment of the Mongol's flexible approach to life. It was both shelter and symbol, its circular shape representing the eternal sky, a central figure in Mongol spirituality.

Moreover, the rhythm and cadence of Mongol life were dictated by the seasons and the needs of their herds. In the spring, the khans would convene the kurultai, a grand assembly where decisions of state were made, alliances forged, and leaders chosen. This gathering was not only a political act but a reaffirmation of the communal values that underpinned Mongol society.

To better grasp the Mongol perspective, consider the words of the great Khan himself: "A man's greatest joy is in victory: to conquer one's enemies, to pursue them, to deprive them of their possessions, to make their beloved weep, to ride their horses, and to embrace their wives and daughters."

This quote not only reflects the Mongol's warrior ethos but also echoes the deep-seated nomadic tradition of seizing opportunities and embracing the transient nature of life.

To truly understand the Mongol Empire, one must see beyond the battles and conquests, peering into the soul of the steppe, where the ger dots the landscape like stars in the night sky, and the thunder of hooves resounds like the heartbeat of an empire built on the move.

In conclusion, the nomadic lifestyle was not merely a backdrop for the Mongols but the crucible from which their strength and identity were forged. It gave rise to a people who, through their mastery of movement, communication, and adaptation, created an empire that spanned continents and left an indelible mark on the fabric of world history.

Religious Tolerance and Diversity

THE MONGOLS IMPLEMENTED a policy of religious tolerance that became a cornerstone of their governance, a testament to their pragmatic approach to ruling over those they conquered. This policy was critical to the empire's internal cohesion and played a significant role in the stability and prosperity of the Mongol realms.

Grasping the gravity of religious conflict is essential to appreciate the Mongols' approach. Throughout history, religious strife has torn apart empires, ignited wars, and led to the persecution of countless individuals. In stark contrast, the Mongol Empire's leadership recognized that such division could weaken their vast territories, which were home to a plethora of religious traditions including Buddhism, Islam, Christianity, and the indigenous shamanistic practices of the Mongol people themselves.

What would have transpired if the Mongols had not pursued a path of religious acceptance? It is not difficult to conjecture that their empire could have been riven by sectarian violence, ultimately undermining the unity that was essential for maintaining their far-flung domains.

The solution was both elegant and practical: a decree of religious freedom throughout the empire. This edict allowed subjects to worship as they pleased, and it extended to the protection of places of worship and exempted religious leaders from taxation. This policy was not born out of philosophical idealism but rather a shrewd understanding that acceptance would lead to stability.

To implement this solution, the Mongols took several steps. They invited religious leaders to their courts, engaged in theological discussions, and even participated in various religious ceremonies. The Mongol khans themselves often adopted religions that were predominant within their regions, simultaneously respecting and ingraining themselves into the local cultures. Moreover, this policy of religious tolerance facilitated the exchange of ideas and fostered an environment where scholars, artisans, and merchants of all faiths could contribute to the empire's economic and cultural wealth.

The efficacy of the Mongols' policy of religious tolerance is evidenced by the relative peace that prevailed across their territories during the height of their power. The Silk Road, shielded under the auspices of the Pax Mongolica, saw an unprecedented era of safe and fruitful trade between the East and West. This period of tranquility and interchange allowed for the transmission of knowledge, technology, and cultural practices across the empire.

But was there an alternative to this approach? Some may argue that a strict, uniform code of religious law could have provided order. However, considering the vast and varied nature of the Mongol Empire, such rigidity might have stifaced the very dynamism that defined the Mongol rule and could have led to rebellion and fragmentation.

Let us, for a moment, envision the bustling streets of Karakorum, the Mongol capital, as a microcosm of the empire's religious diversity. In one corner, a mosque's call to prayer blends with the distant chimes of a Buddhist temple. Nearby, Christian monks debate with Muslim scholars under the watchful eyes of Tengri-worshipping shamans. This tapestry of beliefs coexisted under a regime that understood the potential of diversity.

We must ask ourselves: How did this policy shape the world we know today? Could the Mongols' acceptance of various faiths have laid early groundwork for the concept of religious freedom that many societies value?

Their stance on religion, one of practical tolerance, reminds us that an empire's strength can be measured not only by its military conquests but also by its capacity to unify a multitude of voices under the banner of religious freedom.

Art and Literature Under the Mongols

THE MONGOL EMPIRE, renowned for its vastness and military prowess, also served as an incubator for a remarkable flourishing of art and literature. This period, often overshadowed by tales of conquest, was one where creativity was not only fostered but revered, with the Mongols becoming unlikely patrons of the cultures over which they held sway.

In the throes of the empire's expansion, a distinct artistry emerged, one that was an amalgamation of the various cultures within the Mongol dominion. This synthesis created an artistic and literary renaissance that, while less discussed, was as potent and transformative as their military campaigns.

The claim is clear: the Mongol Empire was instrumental in cultivating a vibrant cultural landscape. This assertion, seemingly at odds with the image of the ruthless Mongol warrior, is supported by a wealth of evidence. The Mongols, though conquerors, were also connoisseurs of art and literature. They recognized that the arts were not mere trifles but vital to the fabric of a sophisticated society.

Our first piece of evidence comes from the Mongol courts themselves. Here, artisans and writers from across the empire gathered, bringing with them the styles and techniques of their homelands. The court of Kublai Khan, for instance, was a melting pot of cultural influences, with Chinese, Persian, and Arab influences all in evidence. The famed Ilkhanid paintings, a style that developed in Persia under Mongol rule, demonstrate this blend, mixing Persian artistic traditions with Chinese themes and techniques, a testament to the cross-cultural interaction endorsed by the empire.

Venturing deeper into this artistic melting pot, we witness how Chinese landscape painting evolved under Mongol rule. The use of perspective and emptiness, characteristics of Chinese art, were enhanced by new ideas and techniques, resulting in works of profound beauty and complexity. The Yuan dynasty, founded by Kublai Khan, saw the rise of artists like Zhao Mengfu who challenged and redefined artistic norms, blending the refined styles of the Song court with the boldness of Mongol culture.

Yet, even as we admire these achievements, we must consider counterpoints. Skeptics argue that the Mongols, by virtue of their nomadic roots, had little intrinsic interest in the arts and that this cultural efflorescence was merely the byproduct of the societies they conquered. They suggest that the Mongols themselves did little to contribute to the arts, merely appropriating the talents of their subjects.

In rebuttal, it is crucial to clarify the role of the Mongols as more than passive beneficiaries of conquered cultures. Their active patronage—commissioning works, supporting artisans, and fostering cultural exchange—was essential to this artistic synthesis. The Mongols were not artists themselves, but they possessed the vision to recognize and harness the power of art and literature as tools for both cultural integration and prestige.

Further supporting evidence of Mongol influence can be found in the literary world. The Secret History of the Mongols, a literary masterpiece from the thirteenth century, offers a unique glimpse into Mongol society, mythology, and the life of Genghis Khan. This work not only serves as an historical document but also as a piece of literature that employed sophisticated narrative techniques and poetic language, reflecting the Mongols' appreciation for storytelling and history.

The conclusion is inescapable: the artistic and literary contributions during the Mongol reign were profound. The Mongols, far from being mere destroyers, were also creators, patrons who nurtured an environment where art and literature could thrive. They understood the value of cultural capital and wielded it as skillfully as they did their weapons.

As the pages of history turn, the Mongol Empire's legacy in art and literature endures, a vibrant testament to the power of cultural exchange. It challenges us to look beyond the battlefield to the quieter, yet equally enduring, conquests of the mind and spirit. The empire's influence extended far beyond its territorial gains; it shaped the very way we see the world and express our shared humanity.

Mongol Women: Roles and Rights

IN THE GRAND NARRATIVE of the Mongol Empire, often dominated by tales of conquest and the extraordinary feats of its horsemen, the vibrant tapestry of its society can sometimes be overlooked. Yet, within this fabric lies a thread of remarkable strength and intricacy—the role and rights of Mongol women. Their status within the nomadic tribes of the steppes and the empire at large presents a fascinating dichotomy when juxtaposed against the contemporary medieval societies of Europe and the Middle East.

What insights can we glean by exploring these roles and rights, comparing them to those of their counterparts in other civilizations? Such a study not only illuminates the complexities of Mongol society but also challenges modern preconceptions of gender roles in the past.

By setting the stage with the societal norms that prevailed, we begin to discern the benchmarks that will guide our analysis. Mongol women, much like their male counterparts, were reared in the unforgiving climate of the steppes, learning to ride, shoot, and manage the herds. This upbringing fostered a resilience and a degree of autonomy that was less common among women in more sedentary and patriarchal societies of the same period.

In the the Mongol world, women were not relegated to the background, as was often the case elsewhere. They managed the home and family, but their influence extended far beyond. In times of war, they might govern in their husbands' stead, and their advice was sought in matters of state and diplomacy. As we weave through history, we find the threads of their influence entwined with the very sinews of the empire.

So, what similarities can we draw between Mongol women and their European or Middle Eastern contemporaries? At first glance, they shared the fundamental roles of motherhood and homemaking. Yet, there is a striking contrast in the Mongol woman's additional responsibilities and freedoms. They were entrusted with tasks crucial to the survival and prosperity of their tribes, such as erecting and dismantling the yurts, managing family finances, and engaging in trade.

Visualize the Mongol woman, standing tall, eyes surveying the vast steppe that is her domain. She is both nurturer and leader, a stark contrast to the secluded women of a Persian harem or the cloistered nun in a European convent. Indeed, these women could inherit property and command armies and at times fight, a concept almost inconceivable in other lands where women's rights were severely constrained.

What does this direct contrast reveal? The Mongol Empire, often perceived through the lens of its male warriors, was in truth a society that afforded its women a status that empowered them to influence the realms of economics, politics, and even warfare.

But let us not be lulled into believing that the life of a Mongol woman was one of complete equality and freedom. They still lived within a framework that valued male leadership and valor in battle. Yet, within these confines, they carved out roles that were robust and respected, their rights enshrined in the very laws of the Yassa, the legal code established by Genghis Khan.

Delving deeper into the analysis, we confront a paradox. The Mongol woman's liberty was, in part, born from the necessity of a nomadic lifestyle, where survival hinged on the contributions of every member, male or female. Their empowerment was not an ideological stance on gender but a pragmatic response to the demands of their world.

Mongol women, in their time, were the unsung strategists, the stalwart guardians of their folk, and often the subtle but undeniable power behind the throne. Their legacy is a reminder that the strength of an empire can be measured not only by the might of its armies but also by the freedoms and roles of its women. How different might our world be today if the lessons of their agency had been woven into the fabric of all societies from that time forward?

The Mongol Empire, in all its complexity and color, reveals a narrative that challenges us to look beyond our preconceived notions. The roles and rights of Mongol women stand as a testament to the empire's depth and diversity, a chapter in history that compels us to question, reflect, and perhaps, to reimagine the fabric of our own societal norms.

The Mongol Legacy in Architecture

THE MONGOL EMPIRE, stretching from the Eastern shores of Asia to the heart of Europe, not only conjured images of fearsome horsemen and vast conquests but also left an indelible mark on the world of architecture. From the steppe lands of Mongolia to the citadels of Persia, the architectural legacy of the Mongols endures, telling stories of innovation, integration, and inspiration.

In the early 13th century, as the Mongol Empire began to sprawl across the known world under the leadership of Genghis Khan, a distinct architectural style had yet to emerge. Nomadic at heart, the early Mongols left few permanent structures in their wake, their lifestyle instead epitomized by the portable yurt. But as their domain expanded, the Mongols encountered diverse civilizations and their architectural styles. What followed was a remarkable fusion of form and function that would echo through the ages.

As the Mongol hordes swept through the lands, they razed many an ancient city to the ground. However, in the rebuilding, they often employed the skilled artisans and craftsmen from these very lands. The ruins of bygone eras thus gave rise to new edifices that bore the imprints of both Mongol will and local tradition. One might wonder, what architectural marvels rose from these ashes?

The construction of Karakorum, the empire's capital in the 13th century, marked a significant milestone. Here, under Ögedei Khan's rule, artisans from captured territories brought their expertise, creating a city that flaunted cosmopolitan flair. Temples of various faiths, including Christian, Muslim, and Buddhist, stood side by side with the grand palace of the Khan, symbolizing the empire's religious tolerance and cultural diversity.

Imagine the sight as you approached the towering walls of Karakorum, the eclectic skyline telling a tale of a world empire in the making. How did these structures manifest the Mongol's world vision? How did they blend the steppe's practicality with the grandeur of the sedentary civilizations they now ruled?

The Mongol impact on architecture is perhaps most evident in the Ilkhanate, a division of the empire in Persia. The Ilkhans, beginning with Hulagu Khan, were patrons of monumental architecture, and under their reign, the Persian landscape was graced with architectural gems such as the Soltaniyeh Dome, still standing tall with its azure tiles glinting in the sun. Here, the Mongols did not merely adopt the Persian architectural style; they enhanced it, introducing innovations such as double-shell domes and intricate Muqarnas.

Each brick in the grand edifices of the Mongol era tells a story of synthesis, where the nomadic spirit met the permanence of stone and mortar. How did these structures reflect the Mongol's administrative prowess and their unquenchable thirst for grandeur?

As the empire fractured and the centuries turned, the Mongol architectural influence melded seamlessly into the fabric of the regions they once ruled. The Timurids, descendants of the Mongols, erected soaring minarets and majestic mosques that continued the legacy in Central Asia. The famed Registan in Samarkand, with its three madrasahs, stands as a testament to this enduring architectural heritage.

In the modern world, echoes of the Mongol influence persist. Contemporary architects sometimes draw upon the empire's architectural elements, reflecting on the interplay between open space and built environment, a hallmark of Mongol design. What modern structures, one might ponder, carry the whisper of the Mongol past within their walls?

Yet, the Mongol architectural legacy is not without controversy. The very act of construction often came at the cost of destruction. Cities were razed, populations displaced, and resources appropriated. In the grand domes and towering minarets, some see not only beauty and innovation but also the shadows of conquest and subjugation. How do we reconcile these two facets of the Mongol architectural heritage?

The Mongol Empire's architectural impact was a product of its time—grandiose, diverse, and unapologetically ambitious. It was an empire that sought to manifest its might in stone and tile, leaving behind structures that compel us to marvel at their ingenuity and mourn their cost.

The Mongol legacy in architecture, much like the empire itself, is a complex mosaic. It is a story of assimilation and conquest, of permanence etched into the very lands the Mongols once roamed. As historians and architects continue to study these structures, they are reminded that the empire's reach extended far beyond the battlefield—it shaped the skyline of history.

The Mongol Empire's architectural saga invites us to witness the rise of an aesthetic born amidst the yurts on the steppes and brought to fruition in the grand edifices that adorned their vast empire. The structures that remain stand as silent sentinels to an era of unparalleled expansion, a legacy carved in stone, and a chapter in the annals of architectural history that continues to captivate and intrigue.

The Mongols and the Modern World

Geopolitical Echoes: Modern Nation States

In the shadow of the once vast Mongol Empire, the modern world map unfurls, a patchwork quilt of nations stitched together by history's relentless hands. The legacies of horsemen and archers, of conquests and khans, persist in the contours of current geopolitical landscapes. Yet, amidst the familiar patterns, one region stands as a testament to the enduring echoes of the Mongol dominion: Central Asia, where the whispers of the past shape the shouts of the present.

As dawn breaks over the steppes, the rising sun casts long shadows over nations reborn from the remnants of empire. Here, amongst the descendants of warriors and nomads, lies a case study of history's reach through time—a tale of borders drawn and redrawn, of conflicts ignited and extinguished, all under the watchful gaze of the great Genghis Khan's spectral legacy.

Kazakhstan, Mongolia, Russia, and China—these are the main players in our story, sovereign states whose modern fates were unwittingly penned on the parchment of the thirteenth century. Each of these nations, with their intricate tapestries of ethnicity, culture, and political ambition, traces a lineage to the era of Mongol supremacy.

The challenge, as stark as the Gobi's cold desert night, is the dispute over resources and territory—a geopolitical chess game with roots entangled in the annals of the Mongol Empire. The borders that once ebbed and flowed with the tide of horse hooves now bristle with the tension of national interests, as each state vies for control over the region's abundant mineral wealth and strategic position.

Strategies abound in this modern contest of wills. Diplomacy dances hand in hand with displays of military might, while economic partnerships are wielded as both shields and swords. The New Silk Road initiative by China seeks to weave these nations together through trade and infrastructure, a move both lauded for its economic potential and eyed warily for its geopolitical implications.

The results of these contemporary maneuvers are as varied as the steppes are vast. Economic growth sprouts like hardy grass through the cracks of political discord, yet the specter of unrest lingers, a reminder of the delicate balance that must be maintained. Data points, like stars in the night sky, plot a course of cautious optimism; trade volumes swell, yet so too do the arsenals of wary neighbors.

One might ponder, what can be gleaned from this intricate dance of nations? The reflection is clear: the shadows of the past hold sway over the present. The Mongol Empire, with its unparalleled expanse, sowed seeds that have grown into the geopolitical realities of today. Yet, the lessons of history are double-edged, sharpened by both the successes and failures of the empire's governance.

Visual aids appear scarce upon the steppe, but one need only look to the maps—old and new—to see the lines of influence. The borders may have shifted, but the connections, the cultural and political ties, are etched into the land as indelibly as the ancient petroglyphs that mark the region's rugged beauty.

To grasp the full picture, one must connect these modern narratives to the sprawling saga of the Mongols. Their empire, a crucible of innovation and brutality, of unity and division, mirrors the complexities of the contemporary world stage. The geopolitical game of Central Asia is but one chapter in a book that spans centuries, a series of events set into motion by the thundering hooves of Genghis Khan's horde.

So, dear reader, what thought shall we carry forth from this tableau of history's enduring grip? Perhaps it is this: the lines we draw on maps are but a temporary order, a fleeting arrangement subject to the whims of time and the echoes of empires long gone. Can we truly understand the present without heeding the lessons of the past?

As you ponder this, imagine the vast Mongol Empire beneath a starlit sky, its legacy a silent whisper in the winds that sweep across the modern borders of nation-states, reminding us that history is not merely a story of what was, but a living, breathing presence that shapes the very ground we stand upon.

The Mongol Image: Perception Vs. Reality

IN THE ANNALS OF HISTORY, few empires have evoked as much awe and misunderstanding as the Mongol Empire. From the windswept steppes of Central Asia, a wave of horsemen surged forth under the banners of Genghis Khan, creating the largest contiguous land empire in history. The mere mention of the name "Mongol" conjures images of ruthless warriors on horseback, cities razed to the ground, and an unquenchable thirst for conquest. However, beneath the veneer of these enduring stereotypes lies a far more complex reality—a civilization that was as much about cultural exchange and statecraft as it was about warfare.

The prevailing image of the Mongols, as barbaric destroyers, has persisted for centuries, shaping our understanding of a people who were instrumental in connecting the East and the West. This distorted perception masks the innovative administration and sophisticated governance that underpinned the empire's vast territories. The consequences of such a narrow view are not merely academic; they influence contemporary discussions about cultural heritage, national identity, and historical narrative.

Should this problem remain unaddressed, the risk is twofold. First, we deny the Mongols their rightful place in world history as pioneers of early globalization. Second, and perhaps more importantly, we perpetuate a cycle of cultural bias that hinders cross-cultural understanding and appreciation.

To rectify this, we must embark on a journey to unravel the myths and reveal the truth about the Mongol Empire. By examining historical records, archaeological findings, and scholarly research, we can reconstruct a more nuanced portrait of the Mongol legacy.

The first step in this endeavor is to scrutinize our sources of information. Much of what we know about the Mongols comes from the writings of their contemporaries, many of whom were from civilizations that had suffered at the hands of the Mongol armies. Naturally, their accounts reflect their experiences and often fail to capture the broader context of Mongol society.

Furthermore, we should amplify the voices of modern Mongolian scholars and historians who offer invaluable insights into their ancestors' legacy. By incorporating their perspectives, we can begin to dismantle the monolithic image of the Mongols and appreciate the diversity and sophistication of their empire.

As previously mentioned, one of the most significant aspects of the Mongol Empire was its unprecedented religious tolerance. In an era when religious persecution was the norm, the Mongols allowed their subjects to practice their faiths freely. This policy fostered an environment of cultural exchange and learning that remains unmatched in history. By highlighting such policies, we can challenge the existing narrative and shed light on the empire's contributions to the advancement of human civilization.

Moreover, the Mongol Empire's meritocratic system and its innovative communication network, the Yam, were revolutionary for their time and deserve recognition. These facets of Mongol governance facilitated trade, diplomacy, and cultural exchange across Asia and Europe, contributing to the Renaissance and the Age of Exploration.

To bring about a shift in perception, educational curriculums must be updated to include a more balanced view of the Mongol Empire. This involves not only presenting the Mongols as skilled warriors but also as patrons of the arts, savvy traders, and shrewd diplomats. Museums and cultural institutions can play a role in this transformation by curating exhibits that showcase the empire's contributions to art, science, and culture.

As we reassess and disseminate this more accurate image of the Mongols, we must also acknowledge the allure of alternative narratives. Some may argue that the Mongol's military prowess and their impact on conquered societies should remain at the forefront of our historical inquiry. While these aspects are certainly the predominant part of the story, they should not eclipse the empire's other achievements.

In conclusion, the journey to untangle the Mongol image from centuries of misconception is a challenging task, one that requires dedication, scholarly rigor, and a willingness to view history through a multifaceted lens. By doing so, we can begin to appreciate the reality of the Mongol Empire—a realm of innovation, diversity, and enduring influence. Let us move forward with the understanding that the Mongols were not just conquerors of land but also architects of a connected world, a reality that continues to shape our global landscape today.

Genetic Legacy: The DNA Imprint

BENEATH THE VAST CANVAS of history, where the grandeur of empires rises and falls, the Mongol Empire etches an indelible mark not only on the annals of time but also on the very fabric of human biology. It is within this intricate weave of ancestry and genetics that we find the subtle yet profound influence of the Mongols' sweeping dominion across Eurasia.

As the dawn of understanding breaks upon the topic of genetic legacy, it becomes clear that the Mongols, in their relentless expansion, left more than just cultural imprints and architectural ruins—they left a trail of genetic markers scattered across continents. The central theme of this discourse is thus to illuminate the genetic impact of the Mongol Empire's vast reach, an exploration that delves into the sinews and cells that compose our very being.

The assertion that stands at the heart of this investigation is bold yet grounded in scientific curiosity: the Mongols, through their extensive conquests and interactions with a myriad of peoples, have left a measurable genetic signature in modern populations across Eurasia. This claim beckons for evidence, concrete and tangible, to either substantiate or refute its veracity.

Our primary evidence emerges from the realm of genetic studies, where the Y-chromosome haplogroup C3*—believed to be prevalent among the Mongol populations—serves as a molecular beacon across the genetic landscape. Recent research indicates that this haplogroup is found in a significant proportion of men in regions once under the sway of the Mongol hordes. The presence of this genetic marker in diverse ethnic groups from Asia to Eastern Europe suggests a common thread woven during the era of Mongol expansion.

Delving deeper into the evidence, we find that the lineage of Genghis Khan himself has been a particular focus of these genetic inquiries. Scientists have posited that the Y-chromosome of Genghis Khan has proliferated to such an extent that it is present in a substantial number of men across former Mongol territories. This hypothesis is based on the convergence of historical accounts that detail the reproductive patterns of Mongol leaders, who often fathered children with numerous women, and genetic data that reveal a clustering of C3* haplogroup variants within these regions.

Yet, as with any scholarly pursuit, counter-evidence and counterarguments arise, casting shadows of doubt upon the initial claim. Skeptics point out that the genetic spread could be attributed to other migratory patterns and historical events, not solely to the influence of the Mongol Empire. They posit that trade routes, such as the Silk Road, and later population movements might have contributed equally, if not more significantly, to the genetic distribution observed today.

In rebuttal, while acknowledging the complexity of human history and the myriad factors influencing genetic drift, proponents of the Mongol genetic legacy argue that the timing, historical records, and patterns of genetic distribution align more closely with the period of Mongol ascendancy. They highlight the empire's policy of moving skilled craftsmen, soldiers, and entire populations from one region to another as part of their empire-building strategy, which would have facilitated the genetic mixing attributed to them.

Further supporting evidence is found in the oral traditions and historical narratives of the peoples of Central Asia, who recount tales of the Mongols' pervasive impact on their societies, not only in culture and language but also in lineage and ancestry. These accounts lend credence to the genetic findings, suggesting a correlation between the historical presence of the Mongols and the genetic imprints left in their wake.

The assertion that the Mongol Empire has had a lasting genetic impact on Eurasian populations is reinforced through a combination of scientific research, historical documentation, and cultural testimony. The genetic legacy of the Mongols, subtly interwoven into the genetic tapestry of countless individuals, serves as a testament to the profound and enduring influence of one of history's most formidable empires.

As the echoes of hooves thundering across the steppe fade into the annals of history, the silent whispers of our DNA continue to recount the tale of the Mongol Empire. It is a story etched not only in stones and scrolls but also in the very essence of humanity, revealing an empire whose reach extended beyond the borders of land and time, into the core of our genetic heritage.

The Mongol Empire in Popular Culture

IN THE VAST TAPESTRY of history, the Mongol Empire stretches across the canvas with bold strokes, its influence permeating not just the annals of warfare but also the rich fabric of popular culture. The empire's narrative, woven with tales of conquest and the legendary figures who shaped it, has been retold and reimagined through the lens of contemporary media, captivating audiences and sparking curiosity about this formidable chapter of the past.

Set against the backdrop of today's fascination with historical drama, one particular cinematic endeavor stands out, an ambitious film that sought to capture the magnitude of the Mongol legacy. It was a production that promised to transport viewers back to the 13th century, to the heart of an empire that once spanned from the Pacific to the Carpathians.

The central figures of this narrative were none other than the indomitable Genghis Khan and his lineage, portrayed with a complexity that transcended the stereotypical warlord image prevalent in earlier depictions. The filmmakers, well aware of the historical prowess and the cultural significance of their subjects, approached the portrayal with a nuanced blend of reverence and authenticity.

The challenge they faced was monumental: to craft a story that was both historically accurate and cinematically engaging, all while navigating the sensitivities of portraying a culture deeply rooted in the identity of many modern-day nations. The weight of this responsibility was not lost on the creators, who delved into extensive research, consulting historians, and cultural experts to ensure their representation was faithful to the source material.

The approach adopted by the production team was as multifaceted as the empire itself. They combined stunning landscapes with intricate set designs to recreate the world of the Mongols. The casting process involved a meticulous search for actors who could embody the spirit of the characters they were to play. Moreover, the script was imbued with dialogue that reflected the linguistic diversity of the empire, with subtitled translations enhancing the film's authenticity.

As the epic unfolded on the silver screen, the results were undeniable. Critics and audiences alike were enthralled by the sweeping battle scenes, the intricate political intrigue, and the human drama that painted a portrait of the Mongol rulers as more than mere conquerors. Box office numbers and accolades followed, signaling not just commercial success but also cultural impact.

Yet, upon reflection, the film was not without its criticisms. Some scholars pointed out historical inaccuracies, while others debated the romanticization of figures whose reigns were marked by violence and subjugation. These discussions opened up broader dialogues about the portrayal of history in popular culture and the responsibilities of filmmakers in shaping public perception.

Visual aids were not merely supplementary but integral to the understanding of this cultural phenomenon. Promotional posters featured the iconic imagery of a lone horseman against the vast steppe, while the film's storyboards detailed the meticulous planning behind each scene. These materials provided a glimpse into the creative process and served as artifacts of the film's ambition to capture the essence of the Mongol Empire.

This cinematic case study, in its successes and controversies, connects to a larger narrative about the power of popular culture to shape historical memory. It raises questions about the lines between entertainment, education, and mythology, and how each retelling of history carries the potential to alter our collective understanding.

As we close the curtains on this cinematic exploration, one can't help but ponder the future portrayals of the Mongol Empire. Will they continue to balance the scales of accuracy and artistry? Will they provoke thought and conversation, or will they succumb to the allure of myth-making? The enduring fascination with the Mongols suggests that their story is far from finished on the cultural stage, inviting us to consider what other untold tales await their turn in the spotlight.

Note to the reader

Thank you for purchasing this book on the history of the Mongol Empire. While some facts may have been lost to time, we have tried to be faithful to the empire that once stood many years ago. Feel free to continue the series, as we continue looking into the ancient empires of the world. If you truly have enjoyed reading this book, don't just leave a review, tell others about it.

Don't miss out!

Visit the website below and you can sign up to receive emails whenever History Nerds publishes a new book. There's no charge and no obligation.

https://books2read.com/r/B-A-ODOK-FMAUC

BOOKS 2 READ

Connecting independent readers to independent writers.

Also by History Nerds

Ancient Empires
The Ottoman Empire
Rome: The Rise and Fall
The Mongol Empire

Celtic Heroes and Legends
Celtic History
William Butler Yeats: Nobel Prize Winning Poet
Robert the Bruce
Scáthach
Finn McCool
William Wallace: Scotland's Great Freedom Fighter

Frauen des Krieges
Boudica: Königin der Icener
Jeanne d'Arc
Irena Sendler

Great Wars of the World
World War 1
World War 2
The Napoleonic Wars: One Shot at Glory
The Serbian Revolution: 1804-1835
Peace Won by the Saber: The Crimean War, 1853-1856
The Fiery Maelstrom of Freedom
The Wars of the Roses

Pirate Chronicles
Grace O'Malley: The Pirate Queen of Ireland
Blackbeard
William Kidd
Ching Shih

The History of the Vikings
Vikings
Longships on Restless Seas

Women of War
Boudica: Queen of the Iceni
Joan of Arc
Irena Sendler
Virginia Hall
Queen Amanirenas

World History
The History of the United Kingdom
The History of Ireland
The History of America
The History of Scotland
The History of Wales

Standalone
Grace O'Malley: Die Piratenkönigin von Irland